for Ma
from And
In Heritage Furniture

DEMONS in the CHURCH

by
Ellis H. Skolfield

This book was originally published by:

Fish House
Fort Meyers, Florida
Under ISBN 0-9628139-2-3

HOSS Publishing
(A division of Home, Office, Sport Supply)
First Reprint, July 2024
Reprinted by permission

Available from your favorite bookstore
or contact:
Home, Office, Sport Supply
2297 Yatesville Rd.
Penn Yan, NY 14527
315-536-8705
Wholesale inquiries welcome

Typeset by: HOSS Publishing
Printed by: Pilgrim Book Printing

Preface to the Reprinted Edition

I was first introduced to *DEMONS IN THE CHURCH*, and its predecessor *SUNSET of the WESTERN CHURCH*, some time in the 1990s by my younger sister Mary Ann (1959-2012). She always remained single because of a congenital heart defect, but she loved to read good books.

The original author, Ellis H. Skolfield, was at one time involved in Protestant Charismatic churches that teach a "second work of grace", or "baptism of the Holy Spirit" doctrine apart from the new birth, and therefore claim to be "Full Gospel" churches. He points out the unbiblical nature of this doctrine, and the dangers of an unhealthy obsession with speaking in tongues and miraculous physical healings. A unique feature of the book is that the author stresses God's order of creation, the proper role of women in the church, and the wearing of a prayer veiling. But he goes farther, suggesting that to not follow God's order in these matters is disobedience and leaves one open to demonic attack. This alone was enough to guarantee that it would never make bestseller status in Protestant Christian circles.

Although I was much impressed initially when I read these titles, they essentially moldered in my library, almost forgotten, for about 25 years. They were brought back to my attention recently when one of my sons asked me if I had ever heard of them. When I dug them out of their long-term cocoons and re-read them, I realized that it was time to re-introduce them to the church as a warning to those who are overcome by the cares of this world, or are preoccupied with thoughts of "...I will pull down my barns, and build greater; and there I will store all my crops and my goods." (Luke 12:18) This problem also applies to preoccupations with other business empires, etc. This can result in a certain forgetfulness of the fact that this world is a spiritual battleground between the forces of light and darkness, and WE are the target of this war – caught in the crossfire of the *War for Mansoul*, as John Bunyan so indelicately put it.

I re-introduce this book to an Anabaptist audience (primarily) that has properly emphasized the righteousness, love, and saving power of God, while I fear at the same time, under-emphasizing the reality of dark Satanic forces that attack disobedient persons who do not obey the doctrines of Jesus Christ. It would be a huge mistake to think that we are immune to these forces simply because our forefathers adhered to the Christian faith, even to the point of death. Jesus scolded the Jewish religious leaders and warned them, "Brood of vipers! Who warned you to flee from the wrath to come? Therefore bear fruits worthy of repentance, and do not think to say to yourselves, 'We have

Abraham as *our* father'. For I say to you that God is able to raise up children to Abraham from these stones." (Matthew 3:7-9) If we disregard the teachings of scripture, we can be subject to demonic attack as much as anyone else.

We are warned that in the end times, "...false Christs and false prophets will rise and show great signs and wonders to deceive, if possible, even the elect." (Matthew 24:24). Also, "knowing this first: that scoffers will come in the last days, walking according to their own lusts, and saying, "Where is the promise of his coming? For since the fathers fell asleep, all things continue as *they were* from the beginning of creation". (2 Peter 3:3-4) These are times of great deception. We cannot slouch our way to heaven merely by being the descendants of believers. Although the author was to my knowledge not of Anabaptist persuasion, and issue might be taken with his style or presentation, we feel the book is Biblically sound and warrants reprinting.

We have re-printed this work exactly as it first appeared, with the exception of the redesigned cover and the scripture references. Originally the scripture references were cited from the New American Standard Bible (NASB), but we have changed all references to the New King James Version (NKJV), because of its more familiar style and better textual reliability. Words in *italics* are not in the original Greek but are supplied by the translators. Any stray references to Bible quotations that do not conform to the NKJV are probably still from the NASB.

I wish to thank the following people for their support of this project: Dan Avery, and Josh and Shelli Rodd, for assisting in designing, formatting, proofreading, and critiquing and Norman Miller from Pilgrim Publishing for printing and marketing. Thanks also to the estate of Ellis Skolfield for granting permission to reprint this work. Thanks to my son Jerry for bringing this book to my attention again, and my wife Anna for her patience throughout the project. Lastly, had my sister Mary Ann not initially introduced me to the Skolfield books, it is unlikely that I would ever have discovered this title. It is only proper that I should dedicate this reprint to her memory

Ivan W. Martin
Penn Yan, NY
July, 2024

Publishers Note
to the 1st Edition

Sunset of the Western Church was first published in 1986. At the time, the author believed that the Lord led him to give that book a different name. But some timorous brethren at a Bible college talked him out of it. The name he wanted to use was "too drastic," they said. Too explosive. Present convulsions within the evangelical church have proven how erroneous that criticism was. As a result, the author is naming this sequel what he was guided to name it in the first place: *Demons in the Church.*

Controversial though it may have been, *Sunset* was well received by Christians of many denominations, and went through four English printings, and one Spanish. In the ensuing years, Mr. Skolfield received hundreds of phone calls and letters, affirming, or asking for more details on the Scriptural principles upon which that little book was based. That is what this new work is all about. It is an expansion and clarification of the biblical precepts which were so sketchily addressed in *Sunset.*

A little of this book will be familiar to those who have read *Sunset,* but most is new. The theology upon which the submission ordinance is based is expanded, and many present-day accounts of demonic activity within the church are recorded. Furthermore, *Sunset* needed updating because letters and phone calls received after its publication gave personal testimonies of encounters with the enemy that should be included.

Glossary

Because this book contains some words that are not part of the everyday vocabulary of many households, we have added a glossary of the most uncommon words:

Channeler: A person who conveys thoughts or "energy" from a spirit being or demon.

Charismatics: Church groups that seek the "baptism of the Holy Spirit", and seek after signs and miracles, such as "speaking in tongues", healings, "words of prophesy", visions, being "slain in the spirit" (where a person falls on the floor unconscious), etc.

Demon Possession: A state where evil spirits inhabit, and sometimes control, the behavior of a person. Believers have the protection of the Holy Spirit and need not fear demon possession.

Familiar Spirit: A spirit or demon impersonating a dead person to act as a "guide" or counselor.

Medium: One who makes contact with the spirit world.

Psychic: (si-kik) A person that is sensitive to the spirit world.

The Book is dedicated to Him we all hope soon to see.

Thanks, however, go to many people. First to the many dear brothers and sisters who shared their spiritual struggles, and who in part made this book possible. Then, to Myrl Allinder, Charles Baldini, Jeff Brannon, Tom Case, Mel Hoelzle, Bob Hughes, Craig Marlatt, William McGrath, Dorvan Yoder, and the many other brethren who read the manuscript for doctrinal or conceptual error. And to those who remained at peace with this flawed servant, even when they disagreed with him.

To Selby Beebe, who spent long hours into the night, correcting grammar and punctuation, to Dayna Hamp for her additional help; and to DTS, a distinguished professional editor, who would have apoplexy if his name were to be mentioned. To a patient and godly wife, who fed and took care of this old bear, even when he was too absorbed in his work to thank her.

A special thanks to those who prayed that the Lord would protect the author while this book was being written; for if the concepts it contains are true, then the enemy would prefer not to see the book in print.

May the Lord richly bless that unnamed brother (3000 miles away) whom the Lord led to defray the total cost of publishing this book

Contents

Deliver those
who are drawn toward death,
And hold back those
stumbling to the slaughter,

If you say,
"Surely, we did not know this."
Does not He who
weighs the hearts consider it?
He who keeps your soul
does He not know it?
And will He not render to each man
according to his deeds?

Proverbs 24:11-12

INTRODUCTION

About Truth

This book is not a debate about your doctrine, or my doctrine. It is about truth. Truth is reality. Reality does not require our support to be true: it remains true regardless of personal opinions. This book is about God's truth. It is about direct commands in the Bible. It was not written to please you, or me. It was written to please the Lord our God, and Jesus Christ, His blessed Son. Jesus is the truth, and walking in His truth is inseparable from serving Him. All lies are of the devil; and to whatever degree we depart from truth, we serve the devil:[1]

> He was a murderer from the beginning, and does not stand in the truth, because there is no truth in him. John 8:44

Either God saw down through time and inspired the apostles and prophets to write truth for the saints of the Christian Era, or He didn't. Either God meant what He said in the Bible, or He didn't. Either every word of the Bible is true, or God Himself is not true, and not worthy of worship.

It is the simplest thing in the world to go to the Bible and prove or disprove any doctrinal position we wish. We stroll through life in the belief that anything we do is alright, as long as we can manipulate

---

1 John 14:6, Ephesians 4:21, Revelation 3:7

? 1John14 doesn't exist

Scripture to support it. But is that kind of biased doctrinal system the truth, and is it pleasing to the Lord? Of course not. That's just sweeping the sin of rebellion under the rug of "theological position." The goal of any true Bible study should be to find God's intent for the believer, and walk in it. His truth may not agree with our chosen lifestyle, and if it doesn't, what then? We should still obey the intent of God's Word, regardless of the outcome. That is what being a servant of the Lord is all about. Those who hold other attitudes delude themselves about being Christians, Matthew 7:22.

In the confusion of this present age, we sometimes forget the nature of Him with whom we have to do, Hebrews 4:13. God is eternally holy and cannot lie, Numbers 23:19. Even as you read these words, around His throne are creatures with six wings. With two they cover their faces, with two they cover their feet, and with two they fly. These covering angels cease not to cry, "Holy, holy, holy *is* the Lord of Hosts. The whole earth is full of His glory," Isaiah 6:3.

But the day-to-day concerns of our short little materialistic lives have distracted us, and the reality of these things has been crowded into a little "Sunday Only" comer of our minds. Our spiritual vision has become clouded, and we interact with this Holy Being through a new temple veil of theoretical theology.

But we're comfortable with this arms-length fellowship. We wouldn't want to get too close to the Lord, in any case. We might find that we are doing something wrong. So we accept as virtuous, a host of platitudes which water down the words of this Holy God. All of us have heard them. Some of us have even used them to defend some doctrine we hold dear which cannot be supported from Scripture:

1. "That verse is open to interpretation."
2. "We're not under law, but under grace."
3. "The Spirit hasn't made that verse real to me yet."
4. "That's cultural."
5. "That's legalistic."
6. "My pastor doesn't teach that."
7. "My denomination doesn't believe that."
8. "I don't know what that verse means, but it doesn't mean what it says."

If we brutally examine each of those excuses, every one can be translated: 1... "The traditions of men are ABOVE the Word of God." 2... "I DO NOT believe God's Word." 3... "I WILL NOT obey that verse." Finding excuses to disregard God's Word is not a new thing for man. Rebellion began in the Garden of Eden, and by the time of Jesus' stay on Earth, disobedience to the Word had become a fine art. The Pharisees were past masters at finding excuses for ignoring Scripture. Nevertheless, rebellion against God was the sin which brought Satan down...and caused the fall of man. In Satan's own words:

> "I will ascend above the heights of the clouds, I will be like the Most High." Isaiah 14:14

Through 1900 years of persecution, and the witness of millions of martyrs, you'd think the church would have learned something about the consequences of rebellion; but it doesn't seem so. We're at it again...

There are some ungodly accounts recorded in this book, and some earthy language is used to describe them. Somehow we have to come to our senses. Somehow we need to come face-to-face with how far we have departed from biblical Christianity.

CHAPTER ONE

The Battleground

One of Satan's goals today is to lead Christians so far from the basic truths of the Bible that they can be brought under the influence or control of evil spirits. Only a generation ago, that idea would have seemed absurd; but now it is a sober reality with which the church must deal.

For nineteen and a half centuries the Western Church has been a bastion of the Christian faith, but now it has lost its momentum. The zeal of the great reformation is past; the martyrdom of the saints of the middle ages is all but forgotten; and the church drifts aimlessly in a sea of lukewarm indifference. In a trans-denominational poll taken this year by David Wilkerson:

> "Four out of five (Christians) told us they were dying spiritually: their churches were dead or dying, and their pastors were so concerned about their own security that they were afraid to offend anybody...
>
> Many hundreds of letters from concerned saints said over and over again, we need to hear the truth – we hunger for straight convincing messages that provoke us to righteousness... but God has shown me there are many who cry for truth who will not receive it when it comes".[2]

---

2 David Wilkerson letter, 9/7/1992, (World Challenge, Lindale, TX)

Sounds unbelievable, doesn't it? But that's reality. Most of us don't have a Bible college background, and are not ordained of men; so we think there is little we can do about it. That's a lie of the devil! That's just what Satan wants you to think. This is not a physical war, and we don't need material weapons, not even a pulpit. We are not fighting against men, but against "spiritual *hosts* of wickedness in the heavenly *places*," Ephesians 6:12.

We are fighting the evil spirits which influence the minds of men. And for this battle, the Lord has provided us with one special spiritual weapon which the church has forgotten all about:

> In this book you will learn that by obeying one little New Testament ordinance, you will stir up a hornet's nest in your church, and be up to your neck in a spiritual battle that *(up until now)* you thought was just theoretical!

And here is what you'll be up against. Careless Bible interpretation, coupled with a misconception of the implacable nature of the enemy, has led to a new kind of satanic attack. A new spiritual covert action against scriptural truth that is meeting with more success than any other assault made against the church during the whole Christian Era. To put it into one sentence: Major denominations are unknowingly flirting with pre-christian mystery religions, the occult, and demonism!

Believe it or not, you can have a real impact against these heresies, no matter how unimportant you consider yourself to be. By obeying just one little command, and without saying a single word to anyone, you personally can start a battle! In short order, the enemy will come against you. Those in your church who belong to Jesus will stand forth, and the servants of the enemy will be revealed. It's easy. But before we discuss HOW to fight this battle, we need to take a look at the battleground itself.

Only a generation ago the church was different. Most pastors were men of God who were afraid to deviate from the Bible. They took God's warnings about departing from Scripture seriously, and the every-day Christian knew the Word so well that the heresies now being openly professed by "church leaders" would have never gotten by the first reading. False prophets were soon exposed, and expelled from the church.

But with the advent of mass media and other time-stealing amusements, individual believers and local pastors are spending less time in the Bible. Instead, for their doctrines they are depending upon commentators, denominational headquarters, or highly visible tel-evangelists, many of whom are openly apostate. As a result, an ever-increasing number of so-called evangelical churches are saying that feelings, personal prophecies, or the charismatic[3] experience can be placed equal or above the Bible itself. That is not a new delusion in the church. The same error was in Germany some 600 years ago:

> Some, calling themselves brethren and sisters of the Free Spirit, acted on the assumption that their own feelings were the leading of the Holy Spirit, and gave themselves over to outrageous folly and sin.[4]

Many of today's "church leaders" are teaching the same heresies. They are servants of the enemy, and by their disregard of the Bible, they have invited a demonic invasion of the church. That would be a reckless statement to make, if it could not be directly supported from Scripture:

> "For such *are* false apostles, deceitful workers, transforming themselves into apostles of Christ. And no wonder! For Satan himself transforms himself into an angel of light. Therefore *it is* no great thing if his ministers also transform themselves into ministers of righteousness..." 2 Corinthians 11:13-15[5]

---

3 Within the confines of this book, the term *charismatic* will broadly identify all who believe in a second "work of grace" subsequent to salvation as evidences by some spiritual phenomenon. The term Pentecostal will identify Protestant charismatics. Because of the stigma attached to the above term, new labels such as *The Third Wave* are now being coined to describe this position. But these "new" movements are still *charismatic* in doctrine, and will be so identified.

4 E.H. Broadbent, The Pilgrim Church, (Basingstoke, Banta, UK, Pickering & Inglis, 1981) pp I12-118.

5 Unfortunately, the Elizabethan English of the King James Version is almost unintelligible to many modem readers. As a result, Bible quotations in this book are taken from the (NKJV in this edition) unless otherwise noted. Since this book is written to the church at large, it seemed wise to quote from a translation of the Bible which could be understood by all.

> Now the Spirit expressly says that **in latter times some will depart from the faith, giving heed to deceiving spirits and doctrines of demons,** 1 Timothy 4:1[6]

Unbelievable as it may sound to some, today there are church authorities who are filling those scriptural shoes, right up to their knees. They are teaching "doctrines of demons". In the past, false doctrines which permitted church demonization were in relatively few congregations or denominations. Now, as evidenced by a disregard of biblical ordinances, these heresies are spreading throughout the whole church. Down through the ages, Satan has fought his most violent battles against the ordinances:

> In the 14th and 15th centuries the fight was over the ordinance of communion. A million saints died for the privilege of partaking of both the bread and the cup.
>
> In the 16th and 17th centuries the fight was over the ordinance of baptism. Millions more died because they rejected infant baptism as practiced by the Roman Catholics, and believed instead that they should be baptized subsequent to salvation.[7]

The full importance of these ordinances, and the reasons for the enemy's vicious attacks against them will be discussed in later chapters. But today, the fight is against another ordinance. The ordinance which visibly displays to the angelic hosts that the church is in submission to the Lord Jesus, through His written Word. Through the seven churches of Revelation, the Lord described these coming errors for us in advance. The key phrase to all the seven churches was: "to him that overcomes." So what was the Lord commanding those 1st Century saints to overcome? To five out of the seven, Jesus brought to light some sin within their own ranks. Some sin within the church itself. So it was the sins within the church that the Lord was telling those early

---

6 In this and many other Scripture quotes which follow: Bold face is added to emphasize some doctrinal point, or to bring attention to a central verse or phrase. No such emphasis exists in the original texts of the Bible.

7 Though the author differs with them, the conventional view of infant baptism held by Evangelical Protestants is totally diverse from the Roman position.

Christians to overcome. A church like each of those apostolic churches can be found in the churches of today; and through their example, we likewise are commanded to overcome the sins within our own church, within our own lives.

> "Nevertheless I have a few things against you, because you allow that woman Jezebel, who calls herself a prophetess, to teach and seduce My servants... and to the rest in Thyatira, as many as do not have this doctrine, who have not known the depths of Satan..." Revelation 2:20, 24 (excerpts).

"The depths of Satan..." the doctrines of demons! In our own day, we are again rebelling against God's governmental order, God's authority; and the church is again playing with the occult. The Lord has given us time to repent of interacting with demons, but we don't want to, and Christian after Christian is unknowingly coming under satanic influence. The enemy has attacked in the same way a spider ensnares a butterfly that has blundered into its almost invisible web. Because Satan is a master of delusion, escape is almost impossible, as he winds his cocoon of false doctrine ever tighter around the souls of the spiritually unwary.

Though Satan is a totally defeated enemy who has no authority over obedient saints, it is now a matter of historic record that demons can enter, and even control, the lives of rebellious Christians. An ever-increasing body of documentary evidence shows that this invasion is far more than just an "influence" or "strong oppression." Grossly sinning Christians can literally have demons in residence. This demonic presence within Christians may not be outright "demon possession" in the classic sense, known to befall those involved with satanism and the occult, but from a behavioral standpoint there is little discernible difference.

Merrill Unger in his enlightening book, *What Demons Can Do To Saints,* used the word "demonized" to describe this terrifying spiritual condition. *The Bondage Breaker* by Neil T. Anderson is a later and more helpful book on the same subject. Historically seen only in Africa, South America, and the Far East, both Unger and Anderson have recorded a number of cases of this phenomenon in North American churches. Pastor Bob Dukes of Mississippi wrote:

> "You will get a lot of flack for saying that a Christian can be possessed. Stand strongly in your position on this one! We are in a

> spiritual battle with Lucifer and his angels, from the establishment on the right, to the New Age on the left.
>
> I have seen clear examples of demon possession by those professing to be Christians. For instance, one young man picked himself up from a standing position and hurled his body upward to slam against a locker which was four feet off the floor, and a foot or so behind him. It left a permanent crease in the locker door. He had other such outbursts of rage. He was thoroughly demon possessed.
>
> The point is this. He was a professing Christian! He was also charismatic. His charismatic ministers became so agitated at my suggestion that a Christian in their church could be demon possessed, that they commanded this young man to stop working with our ministry. They tried to take over instead. After three weeks of attempted ministry, in desperation they threw him out of their congregation; and had him committed to a psychiatric institution. Later, the Lord did a tremendous healing on this young brother. So don't give in to the misguided notion that Christians can't get demonized."

And we didn't. Since *Sunset of the Western Church* was published, many Christians have told us of their experiences with these evil spirits, and several like the above are recorded in this book. Some theoretical theologians declare that Christians no longer have the authority to cast out demons, but practical experience in the field shows that view to be incorrect. We are required by Scripture to help brethren in trouble, and nowhere are we told to leave out those who have unknowingly permitted demons access to their lives. Of all the Christians on earth, those poor oppressed souls need help the most. As Neil Anderson wrote:

> "God has not only equipped you with everything you need to ward off the attack of the strong man, but He has also equipped you and authorized you for the search and rescue of the lives of those who are in the devil's clutches."[8]

Jesus came to free all who were oppressed of the devil, and through His name, the Christians are the representatives he has left on Earth to do it:

---

8 Dr. Neil T. Anderson, *The Bondage Breaker*, (Harvest House, Eugene, OR) p91

> ...And look! The tears of the oppressed, But they have no comforter – On the side of their oppressors *there* is power, But they have no comforter. Ecclesiastes 4:1

> "how God anointed Jesus of Nazareth with the Holy Spirit and with power, who went about doing good and healing all who were oppressed by the devil, for God was with Him." Acts 10:38

But any study of the enemy's activity must be kept in scriptural balance. Some Christians have become mentally disturbed by the errors and superstitions about demonism which have been taught in the churches. We hear that Satan has more power and authority than he really does. That is one of the devil's lies. Satan's power is in the lie... the deception... the trickery.[9]

The truth is that Satan was totally defeated at the cross, and Satan's intrigues are defeated by truth. The truth is that Jesus bound the strong man. It's not a power struggle anymore. Jesus won the power struggle through the nail-holes in his hands. You will read here of the activity of the enemy and his minions; but Holy Angels outnumber demons by two to one, Revelation 12:4, and those guardian angels are far more powerful than anything the enemy can throw at us. What's more, Christians have the protection of the indwelling Holy Spirit.

Nevertheless, there are Christians who have turned away from the simple truth of the Gospel, and have become demon-oppressed. To keep it simple, all who were under direct demonic control (even temporarily) will be referred to as being "demonized."

To protect the privacy of those involved, most names and locations have been changed. Other accounts have been edited for clarity or brevity. None of these reports are hearsay. All the narratives recorded in this book happened to real people, personally known to the author, or are from the written records of credible church historians.

Unfortunately, Christians under demonic influence are not too hard to find anymore... and therein lies the tale...

---

9 William C. McGrath in his booklet, *How Superstitious Preaching Spreads Panic*, (Minerva, OH, Christian Printing Mission, 1992) recounts how an improper emphasis on demonic activity can lead to a falling away from the faith.

CHAPTER TWO

First Encounter

Several years ago my wife and I were attending the Sunday evening service at a local Assembly of God church. For some reason beyond our understanding, after the closing prayer, we stood waiting in the vestibule.

"Let's go home," my wife said.

"I can't," I replied, mystified.

"But almost everyone has gone. What are we standing around here for?" A reasonable enough question.

"I haven't the foggiest notion, dear, but we just can't leave yet." I began to wonder what I was doing there.

"Come on, hon, it's getting late." My waiting wife, usually the soul of patience, was becoming a little irritated.

"The service has been over for twenty minutes."

I looked around. Sure enough, there wasn't anyone still there that I knew. Just three or four people chatting over to one side. What was I here for, anyway? I was beginning to think I had taken leave of my senses.

Finally, about half hour after the service was over, a woman I had been introduced to once, but whose name I had forgotten (we'll call her Sally), walked up to me and said, "You don't know why you are here, but you are here to talk to me... I have a demon!"

I was dumbfounded! Having been reared in the Philippines, the son of missionary parents, I had often seen demonized people. I had learned early in life that if someone tells you he is demonized, you had better believe him. Once, as a child, I had ignored such a warning and had been physically attacked by a demonized woman. That being a lesson not easily forgotten, I now silently asked the Lord for His guidance and protection. Then I asked the woman aloud, "And how and when did this happen?"

"I am a member of the choir," Sally replied. "I was on my way down the aisle to join them on the platform, when this demon physically grabbed my head and throat. He has fixed himself to the right side of my face and neck. Sometimes he seizes me so hard that I can't even pray or say Jesus' name."

It was plain to see that the woman was having great difficulty speaking. She was trying to scrape something unseen off the side of her face, and she looked as if she were in some type of deep inner struggle. Her features were slightly contorted, and she spoke in quick gasps... as if she had to hurry up and get it all said, while she was still able to do so.

We started to pray and a strange thing happened. Sally broke into fluent tongues, without any sign of hesitancy or discomfort. Now this is incredible, I thought. She is having great difficulty talking at all. Sometimes she can't even say Jesus' name or pray; and yet she is speaking easily in an unknown "tongue."

By Pentecostal doctrine, speaking in an unknown "tongue" was supposed to be prima-facie evidence that Sally was filled with the Holy Spirit of God. If she was really filled with God's Spirit, why couldn't she say Jesus' name in plain English? I was deeply troubled. Here was a professing sister in Christ, now in bondage to some sort of evil spirit, by a happening which she herself testified took place in a church at the beginning of a worship service. How could this be?

Finally, my half-hour wait after the service became clear. I was there to talk to Sally. But what could the Lord be trying to show me in all this? Back then, I didn't know what to do for her except pray, so I hurried home to spend some time before the Lord. While praying, a little verse came to mind that I hadn't thought of in years. Like everyone else, I didn't think it was of any importance:

> 1 Corinthians 11:10 **For this reason the woman ought to have *a symbol* of authority on *her* head, because of the angels.**

KJV- power NIV - Authority over her own head

Thus began the strangest odyssey through the Scriptures on which the Lord has ever taken me... a study to learn the importance of physically showing to the fallen angelic majesties that the church is under the headship and authority of Jesus Christ. The Word plainly tells us how to do this. The reformation church knew how to do it. Matthew Henry in 1710 AD. knew how. Matter of fact, until 40 years ago, the whole Christian church knew how. Somehow, in just one generation, we have forgotten.[10]

Contracts and Covenants

Down through church history the Lollards have babbled, the Quakers have quaked, the Shakers have shook... and now a latter-day explosion of tongues, prophecies, and words of knowledge. The historic record of these spiritual experiences is not in question here. What we need to determine is this: Are present-day spiritual phenomena taking place within the framework of the scriptural commands that protect us from demonic influence, and do they have apostolic accreditation? Can we tell if they are of God or demonic in origin? Herein lies the central message of this book:

Christians cannot be free from direct demonic attack, nor can the church prevent a demonic invasion, if we do not obey the ordinances of God that limit the enemy's freedom to attack us!

Today, we put great emphasis in the "spirit," and little on our obedience to the Word. Some pastor teachers give protracted sermons on their hatred of legalism.[11] It all sounds sanctified, but lacks spiritual

---

10 A *Commentary of the Whole Bible;* Matthew Henry, Vol. 6, pp 560-562, 813-814.

11 To those who cry "legalism." it is true that we have been freed from the bondage of the law, Romans 7:6, 8:8, Ephesians 2:15, Colossians 2:14. This does not, however, give us license to disobey the law, John 14:15, 21, 23-24, Romans 3:31, 6:16, 7:1, 7:6, 12:1-2, 1 Corinthians 8:9, 2 Thessalonians 1:8, 1 Peter 1:2. By our walk in the Spirit we may now fulfill the requirements of the law, Romans 8:3-4, Galatians 5:13-16, James 1:21-25,2:10, 14, 17, 24. The church is under the law of liberty, to be sure, but a great heresy today is that this liberty frees us from obedience to God's Word. Unfortunately, some have used their freedom from the Levitical code as a license to sin, or to worship God in whatever manner they like. Though the new covenant has precedence over the old, God's Word is eternal and we are commanded to obey it in both Testaments, 1 Samuel 15:22-23, Psalm 119:160, Isaiah 40:8, Matthew 5:19, Philippians 2:12, l Peter 1:2, 14, 1 John 2:3-4, 3:24, 5:2-3, 2 John 6,9. God is unchangeable.

insight. The Bible is the greatest legal document ever written, and will remain so throughout eternity. It contains legally binding agreements between parties (contracts, if you prefer), known to us as the Old and New Testaments. A Testament is a contract. We have access to God, by His eternal legal contract with us, through the blood of His blessed Son. It is our *Writ of Emancipation* which sets us free from the law of sin and death.

> Thus God, determining to show more abundantly to the heirs of promise the immutability of His council, confirmed *it* by an oath, that by two immutable things, in which it *is* impossible for God to lie, we might have strong consolation, who have fled for refuge to lay hold of the hope set before us. Hebrews 6:17-18

It is God upholding this contract that gives us the way of salvation. It is like shooting ourselves in the foot to say we don't like the system. Instead, we should praise God that He is a God of law.[12]

In any contract where two parties are involved, both have responsibilities. On our side we do what God commands; on His part He saves us, and brings to pass all the blessed promises in the Bible. God did not give us His ordinances just to give the church something to do. Obeying his Word is in our best interest. "Thou shalt not murder, commit adultery, steal," are for man's benefit. We cannot live in peace with one another without these laws; nor can we live in harmony with God if we ignore the laws which regulate our relationship to Him:

> which He worked in Christ when He raised Him from the dead and seated *Him* at His right hand in the heavenly *places*, far above all principality and power and might and dominion, and every name that is named, not only in this age, but also in that which is to come. And He put all *things* under His feet, and gave Him to *be* head over all *things* to the church. Ephesians 1:20-23

> You have put all things in subjection under his feet. For in that He put all in subjection under him, He left nothing *that* is not put under him. Hebrews 2:8

---

12 Deuteronomy 29:10-13, Leviticus 26:44-45, Matthew 26:28, Luke 22:20, 2 Corinthians 3:6, Hebrews 9:15,12:22-24, 13:20.

> If you love Me, keep My commandments. John 14:15

> He who says, "I know Him," and does not keep His commandments, is a liar, and the truth is not in him. 1 John 2:4

In the New Testament era, God the Father has put all things under the authority of His Son. We saints have been commanded to submit to the Lord Jesus in all our ways. The Bible has given us one visible ordinance, and two commands, which show our submission to the Lord. If we do not observe these statutes, we show the enemy that the church is in rebellion to God's law. That opens the doors of the church to satanic influences, or outright demonism.

Those who would suggest that saints cannot be demonized, or under demonic influence, do not have their doctrines in line with the practical experience of missionaries on the foreign field, or with the pastors in this country who have had to deal with this problem.[13] Furthermore, it does not appear that such a view is compatible with Scripture:

> But He turned and said to Peter. "Get behind Me. Satan! You are an offence to Me, for you are not mindful of the things of God, but the things of men." Matthew 16:23

> "When an unclean spirit goes out of a man, he goes through dry places, seeking rest; and finding none, he says, 'I will return to my house from which I came.' And when he comes, he finds *it* swept and put in order. Then he goes and takes with *him* seven other spirits more wicked than himself, and they enter and dwell there; and the last *state* of that man is worse than the first." Luke 11:24-27

The man was empty and hadn't been filled by the Holy Ghost.

There is no reason to believe that Jesus' statement to Peter was rhetorical. Peter was certainly being influenced by Satan, but it would be ridiculous to suggest that he was not saved. The Luke passage then tells us of a man's spiritual house that had been "swept and put in order." Is that not the description of a man who has been converted? Of course. Yet it appears that this man could be plagued with demons

---

13 For an in-depth study of this affliction, suggested books are Merrill Unger, *What Demons Can Do To Saints* (Chicago, Moody Press, 1977) and Neil T. Anderson, *Released from Bondage*, (San Bernardino, Here's Life Publishers, 1991)

subsequent to his salvation. The only way Luke 11:24-27 could be interpreted to refer to a spiritual experience other than salvation would be if a man's spiritual house could be "swept *(of sin)* and put in order" while he remained unregenerate. There is no scriptural support for that position.

The next couple of chapters cover a lot of basic theology, but the principles which permit these demonic attacks must be understood if we wish to know why and how evil spirits have the legal right to enter Christians. They have no such rights unless we give them access by law. To understand the saint's legal position in the New Testament Era, we must first examine some Old Testament types of Christ.

CHAPTER THREE

Old Testament Typology

The Old Testament is full of symbols and foreshadowing of the life of Christ. Prophetic pictures, if you like. These symbols appear as historic incidents, religious practices, or physical objects. Each in some way portrayed an aspect of the soon-coming Savior of mankind. These pictorial prophecies are called *types of Christ.* Here are three different categories of *types:*

1) *An Historic Incident:* Abraham offering his only son Isaac, Gen 22:1-13 is a prophetic *type* of God the Father's sacrifice of His only Son, Jesus, for the sins of the World.

2) A Religious Practice: The Passover Lamb, Exodus 12:3-13 is a prophetic *type* of Jesus as God's lamb without spot or blemish, the sinless Savior of fallen man.

3) A Physical Object: The brazen serpent, Numbers 21:9, John 3:14 is a prophetic *type* of the Cross of Calvary itself.

Old Testament *types* displayed either the office of the Lord Jesus as the Son of God, His sacrifice on Earth, or His authority over the church. Much of the New Testament is impossible to understand without a grasp of the spiritual significance of these *types.* The book of Hebrews explains many of them to us. Let's look at the above examples in detail:

A Historic Incident: This beautiful and moving account of Abraham offering up his only son, Isaac, is a type of God the Father sacrificing His only Son for us. This blessed type is in the form of an incident which took place during the lives of the patriarchs:

> Genesis 22:1-13 (excerpts) Now... God tested Abraham... Then He said, "Take now your son, your only *son* Isaac, whom you love, and go to the land of Moriah, and offer him there as a burnt offering on one of the mountains..." But Isaac ... said, "Look, the fire and the wood, but where *is* the lamb for a burnt offering?" And Abraham said, "My son, God will provide for Himself the lamb for a burnt offering." Then they came to the place of which God had told him. And Abraham built an altar there, and placed the wood in order, and bound Isaac his son and laid him on the altar, upon the wood. And Abraham stretched out his hand and took the knife to slay his son.
>
> But the Angel of the LORD called to him from heaven, and said, "Abraham, Abraham!" So he said, "Here I am." And he said, "Do not lay your hand on the lad, do anything to him; for now I know that you fear God, since you have not withheld your son, your only *son*, from Me."

There is nothing else like this in all of recorded history. This dear elder saint was willing to offer his only son, at the Lord's command. What a beautiful symbol of God the Father's willingness to offer His only begotten Son for the sins of the world. And notice Isaac as a type of Jesus. That strong young man did not fight his father's will. Isaac so trusted his father that he was willing even to be slain by him; just as Jesus "...humbled himself, and became obedient unto death, even the death of the cross," Philippians 2:8

A Religious Practice: The sacrifice of the Passover lamb, about which John the Baptist said when he saw Jesus, "Behold! the Lamb of God who takes away the sin of the World," John 1:29. This type defined how the Israelites were to commemorate the crucifixion, even while it was still far in the future. Though ignorant of its true meaning, for three and a half millennia the Jews have been observing Passover. They still revere this type of Christ, even though they don't understand its significance. Here is the account of the events which took place on the night Israel fled Egypt. The night of the first Passover:

Exodus 12:21-30 (excerpts) Then Moses called for all the elders of Israel and said to them. "Pick out and take lambs for yourselves according to your families, and kill the Passover *lamb*. And you shall take a bunch of hyssop, dip *it* in the blood that *is* in the basin, and strike the lintel and the two doorposts with the blood that *is* in the basin. And none of you shall go out of the door of his house until morning. For the LORD will pass through to strike the Egyptians; **and when He sees the blood on the lintel and on the two doorposts, the LORD will pass over the door and will not allow the destroyer to come into your houses** to strike you."

And it came to pass at midnight that the LORD struck all the firstborn in the land of Egypt, from the first-born of Pharaoh who sat on his throne to the firstborn of the captive who *was* in the dungeon... So Pharaoh rose in the night, he, and all his servants, and all the Egyptians; and there was a great cry in Egypt, for *there was* not a house where *there was* not one dead.

Look at how perfect a *type* of the crucifixion the Passover lamb was: A lamb without blemish blood on the lintel and door-posts (in a sign of the cross) hyssop (upon which the Lord was offered sour wine)... and if you were not under the blood, you died. The same is true today; if we are not under the blood of Jesus, we die eternally. Now meditate on this for a while: Passover was not just for show, or tradition; it did something in the material world:

The Israelites obeyed a typological ordinance....and it resulted in physical life!

A Physical Object: Passover is not the only time that observing a typological command resulted in life in the material world. Later during their wilderness wanderings, the Israelites were again grumbling against God and Moses, and the Lord permitted them to be bitten by poisonous snakes. Considering where they were, those serpents were probably the venomous desert asp: a reptile so poisonous that death was inevitable:

Numbers 21:5-9 And the people spoke against God and against Moses: "Why have you brought us up out of Egypt to die in the wilderness? For *there is* no food and no water, and our soul loathes this worthless bread."

> So the LORD sent fiery serpents among the people, and they bit the people; and many of the people of Israel died. Therefore the people came to Moses, and said, "We have sinned, for we have spoken against the LORD and against you; pray to the Lord that He take away the serpents from us." So Moses prayed for the people.
>
> Then the LORD said to Moses. "Make a fiery *serpent*, and set it on a pole; and it shall be that everyone who is bitten, when he looks at it, shall live." So Moses made a bronze serpent, and put it on a pole; and so it was, if a serpent had bitten anyone, **when he looked at the bronze serpent, he lived.**

What a wonderful *type*. Satan was the serpent, and the venom of sin is spiritually fatal. Bronze represents purification or judgment. Satan and sin were totally defeated at the cross, Revelation 5:12-13. When in faith, we look at the cross of Jesus, all the sins that Satan has tempted us to commit are placed under Jesus' blood, and eternal life follows.

> John 3:14-15 And as Moses lifted up the serpent in the wilderness, **even so must the Son of Man be lifted up,** that whoever believes in Him should not perish, but have eternal life.

In John 3:14-15, Jesus refers to that brazen serpent, and instructs Nicodemus, a teacher in Israel, about the true meaning of that Old Testament type. Jesus shows Nicodemus that the brazen serpent was a type of the cross. Again the point can be made: This type was not just for show, or tradition; it had an effect on the lives of real people in the material world:

> **The Israelites looked at a typological symbol of the cross... and it resulted in physical life!**

Now for another kind of type. Shortly after the Exodus, but early in their wilderness wanderings, the Children of Israel were at Meribah. While there, God commanded Moses to strike a rock to bring forth water for His thirsting people:

> And the LORD said to Moses, "Go on before the people, and take with you some of the elders of Israel. Also take in your hand your rod with which you struck the river, and go. Behold, I will stand before you there on the rock in Horeb; and **you shall strike the rock,** and water will

come out of it, that the people may drink." And Moses did so in the sight of the elders of Israel. Exodus 17:5

That rock was a type of Jesus, the rock of our salvation, struck for us once, at Calvary. The Lord through Paul shows us this type, and also reveals to us that the Israelites in the wilderness were saved through Jesus; that God the Father sees the death of His Son as timeless:

1 Corinthians 10:1-4 ...I do not want you to be unaware, brethren that all our fathers were all under the cloud, all passed through the sea, all were baptized into Moses in the cloud and in the sea, all ate the same spiritual food, and all drank the same spiritual drink. **For they drank of that spiritual Rock that followed them, and that Rock was Christ.**

Forth from that rock came the water of life, to which Jesus Himself referred when He said, "If anyone thirsts, let him come to me and drink," John 7:37. So again:

The Israelites drank from a typological symbol of the Lord Jesus....and it resulted in physical life!

A Broken Type

But what happens if a typological ordinance is disobeyed? For the answer to that question, we go back to the Israelites in the wilderness. Years later, the Children of Israel were again at Meribah and thirsted. Again there was no water:

Numbers 20:3-9 And the people contended with Moses and spoke, saying: "If only we had died when our brethren died before the Lord! Why have you brought up the assembly of the LORD into this wilderness, that we and our animals should die here? And why have you made us come up out if Egypt, to bring us to this evil place? It *is* not a place of grain or figs or vines or pomegranates, nor is there any water to drink."

So Moses and Aaron went from the presence of the assembly to the door of the Tabernacle of meeting, and they fell on their faces. And the glory of the LORD appeared to them. Then the LORD spoke to Moses, saying, "Take the rod; you and your brother Aaron gather the congregation together.

Speak to the rock before their eyes, and it will yield its water..."

So Moses took the rod from before the LORD, as He commanded him. And Moses and Aaron gathered the assembly together before the rock; and he said to them, "Hear now, you rebels! Must we bring water for you out of this rock?" **Then Moses lifted his hand and struck the rock twice with his rod; and water came out abundantly,** and the congregation and their animals drank.

Then the LORD spoke to Moses and Aaron, "Because you did not believe Me, to hallow Me in the eyes of the children of Israel, therefore you shall not bring this assembly into the land which I have given them."

This time the Lord commanded Moses to just speak to the rock. Interesting. why strike the rock the first time, but only speak to it the second? Because Jesus only went to the cross once. It is a sin to try to crucify Him to ourselves a second time, Hebrews 6:6. His one perfect sacrifice on the cross was sufficient for all sin for all time. We now speak to Jesus through prayer, and He answers us. He need be struck no more, ever, ever, ever... through all eternity. Isn't that wonderful? What a beautiful picture of the infinite nature of Jesus' death.

But an angry Moses, that beloved, uncompromising man of God, chided to his very soul by the continued rebellion of the Children of Israel, then committed the only sin recorded against him in forty years. He struck the rock twice, and broke a type of Christ. This typologically implied that the one sacrifice of the Lord Jesus was not a perfect satisfaction to God the Father for the sins of the world...that Jesus needed to die more than once...

Deutronomy 32:48 Then the LORD spoke to Moses that very same day, saying: "Go up this mountain of the Abarim, Mount Nebo....view the land of Canaan, which I give to the children of Israel as a possession; and die on the mountain which you ascend, and be gathered to your people, just as Aaron your brother died on Mount Hor and was gathered to his people; because you trespassed against Me among the children of Israel at the waters of Meribah-kadesh, in the wilderness of Zin, because you did not hallow Me in the midst of the children of Israel."

Heartbreaking! Moses, the meekest man on earth, the lawgiver, who spoke to God face-to-face... how he must have regretted that one angry act. In God's eyes this was extremely serious, and the price

Moses had to pay for breaking that one type of Christ was staggering. The Lord did not permit him to lead the Children of Israel into the promised land. Just one broken type prevented Moses from achieving the goal of his whole life's work! Meditate on that for a while.

Other Types

There are further lessons to be learned from the wilderness wanderings. Bible scholars who specialize in typology tell us that the Tabernacle, Moses, and the high priest were themselves, to varying degrees, types of things in heaven, God the Father, and Jesus Christ.

Other aspects of these truths are that Moses and the high priest, as the governmental and spiritual rulers of the Children of Israel, were earthly representatives of God's authority. As types, Moses symbolized God the Father, the high priest portrayed Jesus, and the people depicted the church. The authority of Moses and the high priest over the people was a symbol of God's authority over the church. When these authorities were dishonored in any way, judgment was severe and usually terminal. Here are some scriptural examples:

Nadab and Abihu, Aaron's sons and authorized priests themselves, offered "strange fire" and incense before the Lord, contrary to command. Incense, as used in the Tabernacle, is usually understood to be a type of the Holy Spirit, or of prayer offered through the Holy Spirit. Were Nadab and Abihu worshiping a false god? Not at all. They were worshiping our own true God, but they were doing so in a false spirit. Nadab and Abihu disobeyed HOW, not who! Fire came forth from God's presence and consumed them, Leviticus 10:1-3.

Later, Korab and two hundred and fifty of the elders of Israel demanded that some of the authority, delegated by God to Moses and Aaron, be shared with them. In this request they sinned against God's own authority, because it was God who had appointed Moses and Aaron. The ground opened up and swallowed them, Numbers 16:1-35.

Notice that the sin in these three incidents was rebellion against so-called "minor" revealed truths. The ten commandments were not involved. There was no idolatry, no murder, no adultery; but in each case judgment was severe and irrevocable, even for Moses.

1) Moses broke a type.
2) Nadab and Abihu worshipped in a false spirit.
3) Korab and associates wanted more authority.

Having set the historic stage, are there New Testament parallels for the church?[14] Is there a governmental line of authority spelled out for the New Testament church? Are there also typological ordinances which must be observed; and if so, is there a price to be paid for ignoring them? It might be said that all the religious ordinances for the Children of Israel were types of Christ and the church:

So also, all the New Testament ordinances are types of Christ and the church![15]

If there were serious consequences for Israelites who disregarded Old Testament typological ordinances; rest assured, there are equally serious consequences for Christians who ignore New Testament typological ordinances. "God is the same yesterday, today, and forever."

Baptism and communion are recognized and obeyed by all. Both have scripturally defined results. However, the ordinance related to the Bridegroom and Bride has been generally forgotten in just the last forty years. It can be scripturally and historically shown that ignoring this one ordinance can lead to a demonic invasion of the church. To prove it, we need to study some basic theology. Avoiding demonic influence depends upon avoiding the errors that permit it.

---

14 1 Corinthians 11:3, Ephesians 1:20-28, 8:8-11, Hebrews 8:1, 5:1-9, 8:1-6.

15 By definition, church ordinances are the physical fulfillment of types of Christ in the individual believer or in the assembly. Being a fulfillment of a type of Christ is what makes it an ordinance. It was true for the Israelites... it is true for us. Some conservative denominations hold that ordinances are primarily outward acts or symbols chosen of God to represent a spiritual relationship to Him. They believe that water baptism symbolizes a prior baptism in the Holy Spirit, and that the Lord's Supper symbolizes the communion of those who have already been born again into the body of Christ. The author broadly agrees, but believes that these observances are more than just symbolic.

CHAPTER FOUR

Battle Doctrine

The true church is fighting for its life today. As was mentioned earlier, it's not a physical battle, but a battle for truth. Our warfare is not against flesh and blood, Ephesians 6:10-13. It is a day-by-day spiritual battle against the deceptions of the enemy. Since God's Word, "the Sword of the Spirit," is the only offensive weapon in our armor, Ephesians 6:13-17, it is reasonable to conclude that we derive some spiritual benefit from doing what it says. Through baptism, communion, and the ordinance related to the Bridegroom and Bride, we demonstrate to angelic majesties, three different aspects of the Christian's firm position in Christ. We display our firm position in Jesus: body, soul and spirit.[16]

---

16 Two books which beautifully expound on these truths could prove to be a blessing: Watchman Nee, *The Normal Christian Life*, (Tyndale House, 1985). Watchman Nee, *The Release of the Spirit*, (Tyndale House, 1980).

The Trinity

No one has split the church over how many parts there are to man's nature, because nobody thinks it matters too much. But every truth matters. Satan is a master strategist; and every error he gets into the church (no matter how minor it seems), he gets in there for a reason. For instance, some denominations are of the opinion that man is two part: (1) body, (2) Soul-spirit. Others hold that we are three-part creatures, composed of body, soul, and spirit, Which View IS right? Well, there is explicit biblical evidence which declares that man is a three-part being; and understanding man's nature is vital, because there is an ordinance for each aspect of man's nature:

1 Thessalonians 5:23 Now may the God of peace Himself sanctify you completely; and may your whole spirit, soul, and body be preserved blameless at the coming of our Lord Jesus Christ.[17]

That's pretty clear, isn't it? In the above verse, notice that the three parts of man's nature are individually spoken of. All major English translations say exactly the same thing. 1 Corinthians 14:15 also supports the division between the soul and the spirit. But there is more:

Hebrews 4:12: For the word of God *is* living and powerful, and sharper than any two-edged sword, piercing even to the division of soul and spirit, and of joints and marrow, and is a discerner of the thoughts and intents of the heart.

Some say that Hebrews 4:12 proves just the opposite of what it says; claiming that the writer of Hebrews is using a hyperbole to show that the Word of God can divide something that is indivisible. That takes us back to excuses Nos. 1 and 7, mentioned in the Introduction. Is it not more logical to accept that the Word of God is so penetrating that the Holy Spirit can convict our spirits, while our willful souls wish to go some other way; thus dividing the faith of our spirit from the

---

17 In the Greek text, the particle *kai* (Strong's No. 2532g), translated "and," appears as: body *kai* soul *kai* spirit, showing a definite division between the three different aspects of man's nature. *Kai* is frequently translated "also." Regardless of translation, in the original language this passage does not lend itself to unifying two aspects of man's nature.

worldly desires of our soul? Anyone who has had an inner struggle against sin should relate to that. What are the names of those two areas in our mind which are locked in mortal combat, if not soul and spirit? But there is still more:

> Genesis 1:27 So God created man in His *own* image; in the image of God He created him...

Man's three-part nature is tied to the doctrine of the trinity itself Since God made man in His own image, if man were only two-part: (1) body, (2) soul-spirit, then God is only two part. Doing away with the trinity is the cultic error of the Jehovah's Witness.

> John 1:14 And the Word became flesh and dwelt among us, and we beheld His glory, the glory as of the only begotten of the Father, full of grace and truth.

Man was created over 4000 years before Jesus was born of Mary. We could not have been made in God's *physical* image, because "God is spirit," John 4:24; and prior to Jesus' birth, the Lord did not have a physical body. It was at Jesus' human birth that He "became flesh."[18] So in what way was man made in the image of God? Well, God's spirit is the Holy Spirit; and we have a spirit. Jesus became flesh; and we have flesh. God the Father is the will, and we have a will. Man's will is in his soul; so the soul is the central aspect of man's being.

All flesh will see death, and our spirits return to God from whence they came.[19] It is the soul that needs salvation. It is through the rebellion of his soul that man fell. When we come to the Lord Jesus, it is for the salvation of our souls! It is our souls, the seat of our individual personalities that Jesus came to save. It is the "soul who sins shall die..." Ezekiel 18:4. It is by submission of the soul, through faith in Jesus, that we are saved. Consequently, we do well to observe the

---

18 Jesus did appear in material form in the Old Testament: Genesis18:1-33, Genesis 32:22, Exodus 33:11, Judges 6:11.22, I Kings 19:7, 1 Chronicles 21:18·30 and elsewhere. These appearances before His birth are called *Christophaneia.* But scripturally, it does not appear that Jesus dwelt within a physical body prior to when "he became flesh, and dwelt among us," John 1:14.

19 Psalm 89:48, Job 34:14-15, Psalm 104:29.30, Ecclesiastes 3:20, Ecclesiastes 12:7.

ordinance that relates to our wills, for it displays the salvation of our souls to all creation (including angelic majesties).

It's Not Just Symbolic

It has been theorized that all church ordinances were instituted by Jesus during His life on Earth. That is just not true. John the Baptist initiated baptism, and Jesus initiated communion. However, the ordinance relating to the Bridegroom and Bride is a *church* ordinance. It could not have been instituted before or during Jesus' lifetime, because the New Testament church (with a different system of worship) was not established until after Jesus was glorified!

> **It would have been impossible for the church to observe an ordinance, before there was a church by which it could be observed!**

This new ordinance, given after Pentecost, was contained within the "excellence of the revelation" granted unto Paul, the apostle to the Gentile church.[20]

1. Baptism *protects* the spirit...
2. Communion *protects* the body....
3. Bridegroom and Bride *protects* the Soul.[21]

"Protects" is not too strong a word. Remember, there were several examples of obedience to typological ordinances or commands in the

---

20 Some very conservative denominations hold that Christian ordinances include foot-washing, the holy kiss, anointing in oil for the sick, and holy matrimony. The author agrees that these are all important statutes for the church, but since these are not related to the various aspects of man's nature, they may not be ordinances of the same type as the three discussed in this book.

21 This concept must be kept in scriptural balance. Ordinances are not a substitute for the Christian experience, and do nothing for the unsaved. We are saved by faith in the Lord Jesus, and by that faith alone. We are not saved by our works, nor by the ordinances we observe. Ordinances are not magic rites that sanctify sinners. They are holy observances that bless Christians who have a right relationship with God.

Old Testament which resulted in life or health for the believer: Passover, the Brazen Serpent, honoring of parents, Exodus 20:12; as well as general references showing that health or life resulted from obedience to God's law.[22]

On what basis can we say that the same principles do not apply to the church? Scripture was written for *real* people, fighting *real* spiritual battles, which have a *real* impact upon the spiritual, physical, and mental well-being of the individual. As church history shows, Satan fights his hardest against the ordinances. Why? Because these statutes are just traditional, or just symbolic? Not at all. Observing these New Testament ordinances does something real, which the enemy would like to stop. Satan wants to prevent the church from putting on some of the armor available to us. Spiritual armor which we desperately need, as the death of the martyrs shows:

> Hebrews 12:4 **You have not yet resisted to bloodshed**, striving against sin.

That's the real physical blood of the saints the Lord is speaking of here. The author is disgusted with theoretical theology. Rest fully assured, the ordinances we obey today will have a *real* impact on our lives. If our beliefs don't work in the real world, they aren't worth doing! Funny about Christians, we bicker over *how* we baptize and debate about *how often* we should have communion; and we lose total sight of WHY God gave these ordinances to us in the first place. We have a wonderful God, and these ordinances are given to us for our good. The church generally believes that God's ordinances are just symbolic, or maybe even optional, thus fulfilling:

> 2 Timothy 3:1-5 (excerpts) But know this, that in the last days perilous times will come: For men will be lovers of themselves... **having a form of godliness, but denying its power.**

That is exactly what has happened. We have mammoth churches, with huge congregations, but we have overlooked the power of the statutes. God's ordinances have power, and influence our physical lives.

We have spent some time on these concepts, grasping them is pivotal to understanding how the church gives access to evil spirits. As we mentioned before, each New Testament typological ordinance

---

22 Proverbs 3:7-8, 4:20-22, Psalm 38:3

relates to a different aspect of man's three-part nature. Let's look at these three ordinances in detail.

Ordinance of the Spirit

Baptism, commanded for all believers, displays the burial of the old man, and our resurrection into newness of life in Christ Jesus. By this act we show to men and angels that we have received Jesus as our Savior and that we have now been placed in Christ by God the Father.[23]

Do you remember how Old Testament typological ordinances did something? Remember how Passover and the brazen serpent resulted in physical life for the Israelites? Well, baptism is not just for show either. Baptism is not just typological "busy work" for the church. From Acts 22:16, it is obvious that baptism accomplishes something for the saints who observe it, and 1 Peter 3:21 shows us exactly what baptism does.

> Acts 22:16 And now why are you waiting? Arise and be baptized, and wash away your sins, calling on the name of the Lord.

> 1 Peter 3:21 There is also an antitype which now saves us – baptism (not the removal of the filth of the flesh, but the answer of a good conscience toward God), through the resurrection of Jesus Christ,

Those verses do not teach that we are saved by baptism. Baptism relates to the conscience. The seat of the conscience is the spirit, Romans 9:1. It is within our spirits that the Holy Spirit meets with us and quickens us. So baptism is for man's *spirit:*

> James 4:5 Or do you think that the Scripture says in vain, "The Spirit who dwells in us yearns jealously"?

Prior to our salvation, all of us were in bondage to sin. When we came to the Lord Jesus, our sins were forgiven; but the vivid memories of our shameful past remain. Though theologians who haven't been there may disagree: anyone who has led a life of sin can tell you that the enemy will attack a new saint through his old sinful memories. That is why Scripture shows that new Christians were baptized at the

---

23 Romans 6:1-5, Colossians 1:13, Ephesians 3:6

same time they were converted.[24] Baptism is instrumental in freeing the spirit from a continuing sense of guilt for those sins committed prior to salvation. After salvation, we don't need to be baptized again and again because we now have the indwelling Holy Spirit who convicts us of any new sins on a daily basis, and:

> 1 John 1:9 If we confess our sins, he is faithful and just to forgive us *our* sins and to cleanse us from all unrighteousness.

Many churches don't baptize right away. They wait six months to a year, to make sure that the new believer gets all his doctrinal "I's" dotted and "T's" crossed; and then (if he is still gritting his teeth, and hanging in there) they baptize him. Amidst all that loitering, Satan is attacking that new babe in Christ through the open door of his stained conscience. As a result, many fall away. Because of the doctrinal stumbling blocks in their path, very few new believers ever learn to walk a life of victory. Here is an example:

> In a little town just north of here, a young pastor led a very sinful elderly woman to the Lord. One night she phoned me; "Brother Skolfield, I have just come to the Lord Jesus. I now have peace in my heart for the first time in 65 years, but my past sins are haunting me something awful. How can I get free of these bad thoughts from my past?"

This troubled woman had a whole lifetime of sinful memories that she needed to have "washed away". I called the young pastor who led her to the Lord, and suggested that he baptize that woman right away, and if there was any reason he couldn't, I would.

Somehow, he failed to do so. Shortly after that, being continually tempted, she fell into some of her old ungodly habits. Though failing to be baptized may not have been the only cause for her falling away, scripturally it appears to have been a factor.

> 1 Timothy 1:19 ...having faith **and a good conscience,** which some having rejected, concerning the faith have suffered shipwreck,

This dear old woman had not (through baptism) appealed for a clear conscience, and indeed shipwreck followed. Now she is alienated from her pastor, and we may never again have the opportunity to bring that

24 Acts 2:38, 2:41, 8:12, 8:36, 10:48, 16:15, 16:33, 18:8, 19:5.

troubled woman to the foot of the cross. May God forgive us. Baptism is a God-ordained procedure, administered to new saints, to clear the conscience (the spirit) of the sins committed prior to salvation. Here is an account from Tricia, a young woman in southeast Florida, that shows what can happen when it's done right:

> My father left when I was 12, and I started doing drugs. As I grew up, I got further and further into the drug scene, and by age 26 was a hard coke addict. I did some terrible things, even aborting my two babies. One day I seriously OD'd on coke. I knew I was going to die. As I was falling to the floor, I told God that if He would save me, I would give my life to Him.
>
> I lay unconscious on my kitchen floor for two days. When I came to, I turned myself in to a treatment center for a month. When I got out, I went to a recital in a church. A man who was sitting in the congregation saw me crying and led me to the Lord Jesus. At the instruction of an elder, I started covering my head right away.
>
> I knew all about demons. I had seen them, and was aware of them in my house. At the suggestion of an elder, I went into every room and said aloud, "Jesus Christ has come in the Flesh; this house belongs to a child of the Lord Jesus, and Satan has no rights here anymore. Evil spirits depart in Jesus' name, and go to dry and waterless places." They did not go away all at once, and I had to do it several times; but eventually they all left.
>
> I put off baptism, because I did not 'feel' that I was "ready". Still, I was obsessed by my past sins. Finally, at an elder's firm insistence, I was baptized. I *literally felt something leave my body.* I don't know if it was an evil presence that left, or what; but I now felt clean inside.

Of the 36 people who went through treatment with her six years earlier (if the author recalls correctly), only Trisha has remained consistently drug-free to this day. She herself would add, "With the help of the Lord." Others from that group also accepted the Lord, so what was so unusual about Trisha? Could her early baptism have been partially responsible for her continued victory over drugs? The enemy tried to prevent it. He tempted her with *feelings* that she was *not ready* to obey "believe and be baptized." Why? Because Satan wanted to keep Trisha's sinful past alive! He did not want her past buried with Christ. That would have taken away some of his access.

All new believers in this country have had some contact with the spirit world through movies, TV, the Ouija board, astrology, or some other occult practice. According to a survey by Dr. Anderson, up to 85% of our young people are demon-contaminated to some degree.[25] Aware of this problem, some brethren now follow a 1st Century church mode of baptism.[26] This is not intended to be a critique of any other mode of baptism; this is just the way these brethren do it. First, they ask the convert to renounce his past life. Then they ask the convert to make a firm declaration of his new position in Christ Jesus. Though these words are not struck in stone, the confession goes something like this:

> "I turn away from, reject, and totally renounce Satan and all his works, and his kingdom, and his angels. I repent of all my sins. I accept the Lord Jesus Christ as my personal Savior, and ask Him to become Lord of my life."

Then, observing the command of Jesus in Matthew 28:19, the new brother or sister is baptized "In the name of the Father, in the name of Jesus Christ His Son... and in the Holy Spirit, Amen." If the new believer is being immersed, he is immersed only once. But if he is being poured over (as was a 1st Century practice), the convert is asked to kneel, and he is poured over three times. Once as each name of God is spoken. The mode of baptism is not nearly as important as getting it done! Don't wait around for church officialdom to approve.

We know of one new Jewish believer who has been waiting to be baptized while an Evangelical Presbyterian pastor wrestles with the "theological implications" of whether or not to baptize him. The man who led him to the Lord doesn't want to baptize the new convert himself, because he doesn't want to alienate his pastor. This has gone on for several months. Meanwhile, by his own admission, the new believer is being sorely tempted by his past sinful practices.

Hang the theological implications! Becoming a Christian doesn't mean that we just say different words, attend a different church, or have a new set of doctrinal beliefs. We actually become new creatures in Christ Jesus. Through baptism, our transfer from the kingdom of darkness into the kingdom of God's dear Son is made visible to

---

25 Dr. Neil T. Anderson, *The Seduction of Our Children* (Eugene, OR, Harvest House, 1991) pp 31-45.

26 William McGrath, *The Didache,* ch.4, vs.1-3 (Christian Printing Mission, Minerva, OH, 1976)

angelic majesties. For this new brother's sake, we need to obey the Bible and get him baptized.

You know, if we as little children would simply DO what God says, most of our troubles would be over. So again: Baptism is a God-ordained procedure, administered to new saints, to clear the conscience *(the spirit)* of the sins committed prior to salvation.

Ordinance for the Flesh

Communion displays that the believer is a partaker in the crucifixion of Christ, that he has died with Christ on the cross, and that he assents to the discipline of God.[27] If we accept our loving Heavenly Father's discipline, it limits Satan's legal ground to demand permission to attack our physical bodies. Now some would say that Satan does not have the right to attack the flesh of believers, but Scripture states otherwise. The Lord gave Satan permission to attack Job's body, and Paul (having apostolic authority) gave believers' bodies over to Satan.[28] Then in Jude, we read about a satanic attack against the body of one of the most sanctified saints who ever lived:

> Jude 1:9 Yet Michael the archangel, in contending with the devil, when he disputed about the body of Moses, dared not bring against him a reviling accusation, but said, "The Lord rebuke you!"

Now you don't suppose for a minute that Satan was interested in Moses' dead body, do you? If so, for what? The flesh of a dead man would be of little value to the enemy. Consequently, Satan probably

---

27 1 Corinthians 11:31-32, Galatians 2:20, 1 Corinthians 10:16-17

28 Job 2:6 And the Lord said to Satan, "Behold, he is in your hand, but spare his life." 1 Corinthians 5:5 "...deliver such a one to Satan for the destruction of the flesh, that his spirit may be saved in the day of the Lord Jesus." 1 Timothy 1:20 "...of whom are Hymenaeus and Alexander, whom I delivered to Satan that they may learn not to blaspheme."

wanted to attack Moses' flesh while he was still alive.[29] Why? So that he could prevent Moses from completing God's plan for his life: recording the law, building the tabernacle, and leading Israel through the wilderness. This attack probably took place at Meriba-kadish. That is the only sin (recorded during the wilderness wanderings) which could have given Satan legal access. Now let's look at a New Testament parallel about an attack on the flesh of believers:

> 1 Corinthians 11:27-30 Therefore whoever eats this bread or drinks *this* cup of the Lord in an unworthy manner will be guilty of the body and blood of the Lord. But let a man examine himself, and so let him eat of the bread and drink of the cup. For he who eats and drinks in an unworthy manner eats and drinks judgment to himself, not discerning the Lord's body. **For this reason many *are* weak and sick among you, and many sleep.**

From these verses, it is apparent that taking communion in an unworthy manner can lead to weakness, sickness or even death. Weak, sick or death? That's the flesh! So the Lord is talking about our physical bodies here; and communion is the ordinance which relates to the *flesh*. In observing this ordinance, if we dishonor the body and blood of the Lord Jesus, we open the door to satanic attack on our *flesh*.[30]

Now our God is a kind and loving Savior. Do you think the Lord told us of the dangers associated with communion so He could punish us when we did it wrong? Of course not. Communion was not given to us for evil, but for good. So if doing it wrong results in

---

29 The Greek word for body, *so_ma* (Strong's No.4983g) defined as "the living instrument of life, whether of man living or dead, or of beasts... is also used of the physical nature..." Vine's Expository Dictionary of N.T. Words, (Bethany House, 1984) pp128-129.

30 Because of 1 Corinthians 11:32, some would say that it is the Lord who is causing these trials. However, none of the bad in the world is God-caused. All evil is satanic in origin. Staying behind the blood, protects us from satanic attack. True for the Israelites in Egypt, Exodus 12:23, true for us. When we fall into sin, to draw us back to Himself, the Lord sometimes permits the enemy to attack us. In that way all discipline of the saints is of God, 1 Corinthians 5:5, 1 Timothy 1:20.

sickness, what do you suppose. Doing it right might accomplish? Correct: good health. This does not necessarily mean that all sanctified Christians who take communion properly will never get sick; but I do believe that the Lord will deliver those who are walking in Him from the "diseases of Egypt," those illnesses which are sin-related:[31]

> Deuteronomy 7:12 & 15 "Then it shall come to pass, because you listen to these judgments, and keep and do them, that the LORD your God will keep with you the covenant and the mercy which He swore to your fathers. ...And the Lord will take away from you all sickness, and will afflict you with none of the terrible diseases of Egypt which you have known, but will lay *them* on all those who hate you."

God hasn't changed. If it worked for Israel, it will work for us. Communion is for the preservation of the flesh. But the rules governing these blessings are the same. For these blessings to flow, we need to do exactly what the Lord told Israel to do, "listen to (His) judgments and keep and do them." Yes, we are under grace, but our Holy God is still a God of law.

Ordinance for the Soul

That takes care of the spirit and the flesh, but there is one more facet of man's nature: his soul. The soul is the seat of the will, the mind, the individual's personality. The soul is what makes the body you live in, YOU. When we observe the ordinance which affects the soul, we limit Satan's freedom to attack the very core of our being, our minds.

Now the ordinance which shows the submission of the soul to the Lord Jesus is best understood through the God-appointed relationship between men and women. The biblical concept of the Bridegroom and Bride. This principle is related to authority: The authority of Jesus as head of the church. Gospel parables show the Bridegroom as a type

---

31 Egypt is a type of the unsaved Gentile world, so the "diseases of Egypt" are probably those infirmities which are related to sinful behavior. Medical science is discovering more and more afflictions which are behavior related, from emphysema and heart attacks, to sexually-transmitted diseases and AIDS.

of Christ, and the Bride, a type of the church.[32] Look at the words of John the Baptist when he heard that all men were now following Jesus:

> John 3:28-29 "You yourselves bear me witness, that I said, 'I am not the Christ,' but, 'I have been sent before Him.' **He who has the bride is the bridegroom;"**

So John called Jesus the Bridegroom, and those who followed Him, the Bride. There is further confirmation of this in Isaiah, the gospels, the epistles, and in Revelation.[33] The husband is a type of Christ, the wife a type of the church. The Lord fully spells out these basic truths to us in Ephesians:

> Ephesians 5:22-32 Wives, submit to your own husbands, **as to the Lord.** For the husband is the head of the wife, **as also Christ is head of the church;** and he is the savior of the body. Therefore **just as the church is subject to Christ,** so *let* the wives *be* to their own husbands in everything.
>
> Husbands, love your wives, just as Christ also loved the church and gave himself for her, that he might sanctify and cleanse her with the washing of water by the word, that he might present her to himself a glorious church, not having spot or wrinkle or any such thing, but that she should be holy and without blemish. So husbands ought to love their own wives as their own bodies; he who loves his wife loves himself. For no one ever hated his own flesh, but nourishes and cherishes it, just as the Lord *does* the church. For we are members of his body, of his flesh and of his bones. "For this reason a man shall leave his father and mother and be joined to his wife, and the two shall become one flesh."
>
> **This is a great mystery. but I speak concerning Christ and the church.**

Husband, you are a type of Christ! Wife, you are a type of the church! These truths will stand as long as there are men and women. Notice that phrases like "as unto the Lord," or "as Christ loved the church," appear six times. The Lord wants to make this principle

32 Matthew 9:14-17, 25:1-13, Luke 5:34-35

33 Isaiah 62:5, Matthew 9:15, Matthew 25:5-13, Mark 2:19-20, Luke 5:35, 2 Corinthians 11:2, Romans 7:14, Revelation 18:23, Revelation 21:2,9.

abundantly clear. Now read the last verse again; then again; then one more time. Keep on reading it until the Holy Spirit makes it real to your heart. Husband, you are a type of Christ! Wife, you are a type of the church![34] Unmarried Christian men still appear to be a type of Christ, and unmarried Christian women still appear to be a type of the church. Marital status does not seem to be a factor in this type.[35]

Now the type of the Bridegroom and Bride has one ordinance and two additional commands which display the submission of the church to the headship of Christ. If we ignore the ordinance which shows God's authority, do not think for a moment that it will escape the notice of Satan and his angels. Neither will we be able to remain free of his influence or oppression. There are numerous verses which support this conclusion.[36] So what is this ordinance, and how does it display the authority of God?

---

34 The Bridegroom and Bride is a type of the relationship between Christ and the church in both love and authority. It also regulates how husbands and wives should interact. Nevertheless, it is not an ordinance. Instead it is the theological foundation upon which the ordinance relating to Christ's authority over the church is based. Ordinances are rules of behavior observed by an individual believer, or by an assembly of believers. As was true of Old Testament ordinance's, it appears that a material object was employed in their observance: baptism uses water, communion uses bread and wine, and Bridegroom and Bride uses cloth.

35 Genesis 3:15-16; 1 Corinthians 11:3,7; 1 Timothy 2:9-12. Despite modern practice to the contrary, this typological position cannot be interpreted to mean that unmarried Christians have the liberty to live together without taking marriage vows. In God's eyes, fornication is still sin.

36 1 Corinthians 5:5, 2 Corinthians 2:11, 1 TI 1:20, 5:15, Matthew 12:43-45, Luke 11:24-26, Revelation 2:24, 3:9

CHAPTER FIVE

Who Says It's Legalistic?

Women play an extremely important, and totally ignored, role in the church. Their stand in the Lord is vital to the spiritual health of the church.

> As a type of the church, women have the awesome responsibility of showing the spiritual condition of the church to the unseen spirit world!

By what Christian sisters do, they show to angelic majesties whether or not the church will be under the protection of Holy Angels, or open to demonic attack. In later chapters we will see how some of the saints who ignored this ordinance were demonized.

Now this is where we are going to get into an argument about whether the Bible is the Word of God, or not. About whether God means what He says, or not; and whether what He says is true, or not. This is where we are going to hear all eight "excuses," mentioned in Chapter 1. The typological ordinance relating to the Bridegroom-Bride, and the two supporting commands are as follows:

Ordinance

> 1 Corinthians 11:5-6 **...every woman who prays or prophesies with *her* head uncovered dishonors her head, for that is one and the same as if her head were shaved.** For if a woman is not covered, let her also be shorn. But **if it is shameful for a woman to be shorn or shaved, let her be covered.**

Commands

> 1 Corinthians 14:34 **Let your women keep silent in the churches, for they are not permitted to speak;** but *they* are to be submissive, as the Law also says.

> 1 Timothy 2:12 And **I do not permit a woman to teach or to have authority over a man,** but to be in silence.[37]

Technicalities aside, these are very pointed and explicit statutes, and the Lord did not put them in His Word to be argued over in committee. If you don't like them, your fight is not with the author of this book, but with the Word of God. These commands have been in Scripture for almost 2,000 years, and until this generation they were almost universally observed. If these precepts were not part of God's eternal for the church, they would have been nullified somewhere else in Scripture (just as the Levitical code was superseded by the new covenant). But these commands have not been set aside anywhere, so

---

37 There is a difference between the ordinance of 1 Corinthians 11:5-6, and the submission commands associated with it. The head-covering ordinance is a positive typological act we are ordered to observe. The associated commands are symbolic acts we are ordered NOT to do. Why? Because to disobey them would nullify the typological significance of the ordinance itself. The submission of the church is what this ordinance is all about.

they stand today.[38] Though the connection may not be readily apparent, if we wish to see the church free of demonic influence, we need to see why these commands were given to us, and understand what effect they have on the unseen spirit world.

Believing that the Lord inspired the books of the Bible in the order in which they have been passed down to us, passages relating to these commands are quoted in the order they appear in Scripture. There are many other allusions and quotations, but these are the primary references. The 1st Corinthians passage is quoted in its entirety, to preclude any contention that verses were taken out of context to prove a doctrinal point, or to avoid "difficult" verses. Verses central to our study have been set in bold-face type. Note that all of the commands are stated as firm directives, not suggestions. For a complete exegesis of every verse, see the exegetical note at the end of the chapter.

The Ordinance of Head-Covering

> 1 Corinthians 11:3-19 But I want you to know that the head of every man is Christ, the head of woman is man, and the head of Christ *is* God.
> 4 Every man praying or prophesying having *his* head covered, dishonors his head.
> 5 But **every woman who prays or prophesies with *her* head uncovered dishonors her head, for that is one and the same as if her head were shaved.**
> 6 **For if a woman is not covered, let her also be shorn. But if it is shameful for a woman to be shorn or shaved, let her be covered.**
> 7 For a man indeed ought not to cover his head, since he is the image and glory of God; but woman is the glory of man.
> 8-9 For man is not from woman, but woman from man. Nor was man created for the woman, but woman for the man.
> 10 For this reason **the woman ought to have a *symbol* of authority on *her* head, because of the angels.**
> 11-12 Nevertheless, neither *is* man independent of woman, nor woman independent of man, in the Lord. For as woman *came* from man, even so man also *comes* through woman; but all things are from God.
> 13-16 Judge among yourselves. Is it proper for a woman to pray to God with head uncovered? Does not even nature itself teach you that if a man has long hair, it is a dishonor to him? But if a woman has long

38 2 Peter 3:2, 2 Timothy 3:16-17.

> hair, it is a glory to her; for *her* hair is given to her for a covering. But if anyone seems to be contentious, we have no such custom, nor *do* the churches of God.
> 17-19 Now in giving these instructions I do not praise *you*, since you come together not for the better but for the worse. For first of all, when you come together as a church, I hear that there are divisions among you, and in part I believe it. For there must also be factions among you, that those who are approved may be recognized among you.

Some folks just read over the above passage entirely. Others avoid it like it had smallpox, but by the time we get to v.20, everyone believes we're back in God's Word again. Ahhh, from v.20 on through the rest of the chapter, we are reading about communion. We can live with that; it goes along with our doctrine. So how does the church deal with 1 Corinthians 11:5-6? Why, that's easy enough to handle. To the original eight "excuses" mentioned in the Introduction, nine more are added:

9. "I'll pray about it."
10. "That's for the 1st Century Corinthians."
11. "Oh, that's just Paul, and he didn't like women."
12. "I haven't been convicted of that yet."
13. "My hair is my covering."
14. "My husband is my covering."
15. "That's just spiritual, and not a literal covering."
16. "Only Corinthian harlots went around with their heads uncovered."
17. "I'm a prophetess, and the spirit has not revealed that to me yet."

The author has heard every one of those 17 excuses many times, and if he has missed any, please write, so they can be added to the list. God addressed them all in 2 Timothy 3:16-17 and 2 Peter 3:15-16. Making excuses for rebellion is as old as man, Genesis 3:12, and is sin with a capital "S." It is with the enemy's blessing that we delude ourselves. God isn't fooled. Those excuses just cloak our defiance with argument ("If anyone is inclined to be contentious," 1 Corinthians 11:16). But just as we couldn't understand being born again until we were, neither can we understand the spiritual significance of head-covering, silence, or submission to the authority of the Word until we obey and become submitted:

James 1:22 But be doers of the word, and not hearers only, deceiving yourselves.

So one has to ask: Which of the 17 "excuses" influenced you or your wife to disobey God's Word? Did you know that there is not a shred of historic or documentary evidence for any of them? Some of them are ludicrous. For instance: the Greek text declares that this is a physical, not a "spiritual" covering. For the husband to be a physical covering, he would have to perch on his wife's head like some strange species of flightless bird. Then look at pictures of old Greek pottery. Did Greek women have their heads covered in their art? Not at all. Greek art shows that neither men nor women covered their heads as a daily practice.

Besides all that, church history gives a very clear picture of how the early believers behaved. Drawings in the Catacombs from AD100 invariably showed Christian sisters with their heads covered, and many early church elders affirmed head-covering in their writings. Notable examples are: Clement of Alexandria (AD150-220); Tertullian (?-AD200); Hippolytus (?AD236); Chrysostom (AD344-307); Jerome (AD345-429); and of course Augustine of (AD354-430).[39]

God's Government

Now look carefully at v.3. As that verse itself states, it is the key to understanding this whole passage: "I want you to understand." God the Father is showing to all creation His governmental order. He is the head of Christ, Christ is the head of man, man is the head of woman.

Is this sign only for us here on Earth? Study v.10. God's governmental order is being displayed to angelic majesties. Ephesians 1:18-23 affirms that truth. When a woman, as a type of the church, covers her head, she is showing *to angels* the submission of the church to God's Son. *That is who this ordinance is for, the angels!* 1 Corinthians 11:10. Satan and his angels were totally defeated at the cross, and a public display of that victory is made with a seemingly "little" thing like a woman covering her head.[40]

---

39 Tom Shank, *"let her be veiled"* (Eureka, MT, Torch Publications, 1991) pp4S-49. David Bercot, *Common Sense* (Tyler, TX, Scroll Publications, 1992) pp65-68.

40 Luke 10:18, John 12:31

1 Corinthians 6:3 **Do you not know that we shall judge angels?**

Even theologians don't fully understand God's purpose in all this. But before Satan fell, he was one of the cherubs which covered God's throne, Ezekiel 28:14. Then Satan committed an act of rebellion. He sinned against God's authority. In his own words, "I will make myself like the Most High," Isaiah 14:14. That statement is the ultimate in rebellion, the most monstrous blasphemy. From his position of perfection, he chose to rebel against his creator! Satan led a third of the angels, and all mankind to rebel with him, Revelation 12:4. After Adam fell, all mankind was bound in slavery to sin, and without hope.

Then came Jesus, and from the depths of sin, we turned unto God. We submitted to the authority of Him against whom Satan rebelled. We turned away from our rebellion against God, and turned unto Him through His Son. We accepted the blood of Jesus as the full satisfaction to God the Father for our sins... the full purchase price needed to buy us out of the kingdom of darkness, and transfer us into the glorious kingdom of God's dear Son.[41] These saints will judge angels.

Now you don't suppose that we are going to be sitting up there in heaven, with a gavel in our hands, holding court over Satan and his angels do you? Not likely. He with "the voice of many waters," with "eyes like flaming fire," who sits upon the throne of heaven is the only righteous judge, Revelation 20:11-12. What we have here is the EVIDENCE by which God will judge those fallen angelic majesties; and the evidence is this: Satan, from a state of perfection, rebelled... we, who were in rebellion, submitted to God:

It is that act of submission which judges Satan! Through head-covering, women, as a type of the church, visibly display that submission! They visibly show "to the angels" the submission of the church to Jesus Christ! 1 Corinthians 11:10

That's what it's all about; and that's why Satan so hates for the church to observe this ordinance. It is a visible sign of his defeat and ultimate judgment. And he will do all he can to stop it! That is no joke, as a letter from a pastor's wife in Missouri shows:

"When my husband accepted the pastorate of Bull Creek Church, he made our position clear, that we upheld the 1st Corinthians verses

41 Ephesians 5:8, Colossians 1:13-14, 1 Peter 2:9, 1 Corinthians 1:27.

on woman's head-covering. At the time, there was no objection from the congregation.

The church began to grow, and new families were added. One new family accused us of legalism and bondage. As this family started to attend regularly, we found ourselves struggling with a dying church. Those of our friends who had been growing in knowledge and obedience, began to withdraw from us, and from the Lord. We soon felt led of the Spirit to move on. My husband set a date for his resignation, and prepared his letter.

Unaware of our intent, just days before my husband was to resign, a board member asked him, "Just where do you stand on the covering?" Another one said, "Something has to go, either you or that covering." A third called to inform us that a pastoral review had been requested, and would be held Monday. My husband moved his resignation up to Sunday.

That Sunday my husband preached a short sermon and read his resignation letter. We expected some tears, a few hugs, and a sad farewell. Instead, angry church members swooped down on us like vultures. Fists clenched, spouting words of hate, they accused us of teaching bondage, of being heretics, and of promoting the "false doctrine of the covering." Scriptural views were attacked in a venomous manner. The attacks were so fierce that I believe they would have stoned us, had it been legal to do so."

One doesn't need to wonder who sent those wolves into that church. They came clothed in sheep's clothing, and rent the flock, just as the Lord warned us they would, Acts 20:29. Were those Missouri wolves demon-influenced? It is impossible to believe otherwise. How about the rest of the people in that church, were they saved? Good question. The Pharisees who stoned Stephen acted exactly the same way, Acts 7:54; and were they saved? Only the Lord knows, but the people at Bull Creek weren't guided by the Holy Spirit of God, that's for sure:

Galatians 5:22-24 ...the fruit of the Spirit is love, joy, peace, longsuffering, kindness, goodness, faithfulness, gentleness, self-control. Against such there is no law.

Important as it may be, putting on a head-covering does notaccomplish submission to the Lord Jesus, any more than being baptized or taking communion makes us Christians. The veil or head-covering is just an *outward* sign of the condition of the soul. It is the soul which was lost, and it is the soul that Jesus came to save. So the covering is a sign to the fallen angels of the salvation of a person's soul. Again:

> Head-covering is a visible sign of the salvation of the soul, seen by fallen angels and demons.

That ought to warn us of something! If demons do not see that outward sign, what can they conclude: That the woman not covered is either *a disobedient Christian, or someone who is not saved!* In either case... access! The enemy has been given legal grounds to attack.[42] But attack what? Well, what does that ordinance relate to? The soul, the mind, the will! The very part of your being which makes you an individual! Obeying that ordinance appears to lessen the enemy's freedom to attack your mind. I don't know how it does, but I do know what the brethren tell me. Several years ago, the author was teaching a Bible class in another city. Kathy was hosting that class:

> I am a registered nurse, with two children in their late teens. I didn't come from a Christian family, so I don't know a whole lot about the Bible. I am a divorced single parent, who over time, got into drugs and alcohol. I eventually became an alcoholic. I also had a lot of 'men friends', with new ones coming along every few days. My children were sleeping around, and into drugs and the occult.
>
> Then the Lord saved me, and my whole life changed. I now hate what I used to do for fun. However, my family was still a wreck. The children were rebellious, and I was afraid they were going to go down the road that I had been on. You saw the black-light and satanic stuff in my son's room, and heard my daughter's rage. I was having the worst time imaginable with them. In that atmosphere, the temptations to return to my old life were unreal.

42 There are those who are ignorant of this statute, and "...where there is no law there is no transgression," Romans 4:15. Scripture shows that God is gracious to those who are honestly ignorant of His law, and will protect them. However, when demons see a woman with an uncovered head, they will likely come to the conclusions stated above.

Then I asked you to teach a Bible class to an AA group that met at my house. I told you about all this, and you said for me to cover my head. I thought you were nuts. But you said to try it for 90 days anyway. If it didn't make a difference in my spiritual life, you said to take it off and throw it at you, and tell everyone I knew that you were a fraud and a charlatan.

Well, I tried it like you said, and it didn't take 90 days. In just two weeks you couldn't have pried that hat off my head! The horrible feeling of oppression left me. The temptations were easier to live with, and my home got more peaceful. You wouldn't believe it. My children even went to treatment.

Shortly after that, Kathy moved without leaving a forwarding address, so the author doesn't know the end of her story. By now, some pompous theologian has probably convinced her that head-covering (which benefited her so much) was legalistic or old-fashioned. Maybe Kathy has been turned aside by one of the other 17 excuses. Without the fellowship of like-minded brethren, it would be a miracle if she is still hanging in there. May the Lord be gracious unto her.

Another account, written by a Mennonite sister (edited here for brevity) shows how observing this ordinance can cause a disturbance in the spiritual world. Kay Miller tells of working with a young girl who came from a broken home, had been abused as a child, and was addicted to rock music. At a special meeting, this young lady came to the Lord and her repentance appeared genuine. Then she was asked about wearing a head-covering:

"She was full of doubts and fears at the very suggestion, so we didn't press the issue. But the turmoil within her continued. One moment she wanted to, the next moment she didn't. Somehow she couldn't seem to lay the thought aside. Finally, on her own, she asked for the veiling, and when one of the sisters put it on her, she began to cry.

I asked her, 'Don't you want to wear it?' She insisted that she did, so I asked her, 'Then why are you crying?' She didn't know why – only that she felt so frightened. We asked if we should take it off, and she said, "No," then, "Yes," and then she didn't know. We decided to pray for her, and asked the Lord to give her peace and joy about this – like the joy she had when she first realized that her sins were forgiven.

But her crying continued, and her sobs became more violent. Finally we decided to take the veiling off. Her violent crying stopped, but she

> was not at all happy; in fact, she was miserable.
>
> I talked with her a while, and gave her a hug. She began to cry again, and clung to me almost frantically. I said to her bluntly, 'You will just have to tell Satan to leave you alone, in Jesus name,' not knowing why I said it, or that I was going to. She took me literally and said it out loud. Then she began to scream it out with such violence that some of the sisters went after the brothers to help us.
>
> While everyone gathered in prayer she was delivered from Satan's control. She became a different person. She asked for the veiling again, and this time her face was radiant, and there was no fear. The power of wearing the veiling is evident. Even the demons tremble before it."[43]

That young lady was obviously oppressed by an evil spirit, even after she was saved. Wearing the covering appears to have exposed that hidden enemy. But God's ordinances are not anything to play with. I have heard of some sisters who (like Reuben, Genesis 49:3-4) are unstable as water, putting on and taking off their head-covering depending on the company they keep. Demons see it, and take advantage of people who are that irresolute. Pauline McDowell writes about her friend Jill:

> "Jill is heavy on my heart. When she first came here, she was a head-covering saint. I was drawn to her because of her peace and joy. I saw in her something I wanted in my own life. I watched her remove her head-covering, and begin dressing like the world. She turned into a very unhappy person, even unsure of her own salvation. I watched food become her god, and, when she planned to commit suicide, I personally got her in touch with a mental health person. Jill, in her search for freedom from legalism, has put herself in bondage."

There was nothing wrong with Jill's mind, and she didn't need psychiatric help. She was under spiritual attack because she had knowingly gone against the Bible. Her disobedience had given demons an open door through which they could oppress her soul.

And by now you may be saying, "Skolfield, you sure are making an awfully big deal about just one little statute, and two teensy little commands which appear in only two epistles!" Maybe, but when we stand before the Lord of glory, I can hardly imagine Him saying,

---

43 Tom Shank, "*Let her be veiled*" (Eureka, MT, Torch Publications, 1991) pp71-73.

"You mean to say you took My Word literally? Really, Ellis... don't you think you have over obeyed?" Absurd of course, but better to hear Him say something like that than...

To see His eyes like fire burning,
To hear His voice like thunder saying:
"Why did you not obey My Word?
Stand over there with the goats."[44]

---

44 Several Months after the publication of the 1st edition of *Sunset of the Western Church*, the author received a phone call, then a little book from a William McGrath. A few pages had sentences and paragraphs that were almost word for word duplicates of some of the doctrine that is written in the first few chapters of this book. We had never heard of each other, nor was Mr. McGrath's prior work known to the author. What a wonderful example of how the Holy Spirit will open the truths of Scripture to all, if we would only go to the Lord with a teachable heart.

Mr. McGrath's work, *Woman's Veiling, a Christian and Historic Review,* is replete with illustrations and pictures of different modes of head-coverings from the 1st century on. This interesting work may be purchased from its author for $2.00 postpaid: William McGrath, 8117 Magnet Road, Minerva, Ohio, 44657. Other good works on the subject include, David Bercot, *Common Sense,* (P.O. Box 122, Amberson, PA, 17210, Scroll Publishing Co.) and; Tom Shank, *"Let her be veiled,"* (1484 Hwy. 93N, Eureka, MT 59917, Torch Publications)

EXEGETICAL NOTE

1st Corinthians 11:3-16

1st Corinthians 11:8-16 is impossible to understand apart from the governmental order expressed in V:8, and the significance of men and women as types of Christ and the church, Ephesians 5:32. However, when viewed in that context every verse becomes quite clear.

v.4 Christ is "...above... every name that is named, not only in this age but also that which is to come," Ephesians 1:19-28. As a type of Christ, man's uncovered head shows Jesus' authority over the church. 1 Corinthians 11:4 is not about hair. If it were, then only bald men could pray or prophesy. Since v.4 is not about hair, then neither is v.5 and v.6. Verse 4 is connected to vs.5-6 by the conjunction "but". The Greek connective or adversative particle, *de* (Strong's No.1161g, defined "now") is used here in the antithesis.

vs.5-6 The church should be totally obedient to Jesus. When a woman covers her head she typologically shows the church's submission to the Lord. Greek scholars state that the command for woman's head-covering is expressed in the strongest imperative tense in the Greek language. It is not stated as a suggestion. It is commanded in the most absolutely imperative way available in the Greek language. Why? Paul knew, and expressed it quite clearly:

If a woman does not cover her head, she shows the church's rebellion to the headship of Jesus Christ. The Greek word here is *katakalupto_* (Strong's No.2619g, defined as "to cover up." It implies a veil, or something coming down over the head). That her hair is *not* her cover is proven by, "...let her also be shorn" stated as a command. She must either have her head covered (by something other than her hair) or she must be bald. Head shaving for woman is a universal and timeless symbol for harlotry, and in the OT, harlotry was used symbolically to show idolatry, and a falling away from God. The Lord is letting us know how serious this is. If a woman does not cover her head, she is showing the church to be in spiritual harlotry… in idolatry... in rebellion!

v.7-9 Typologically, the church is to glorify Jesus... not Jesus the church. The church originates from Jesus... not Jesus from the church. The church was created for Jesus... not Jesus for the church.

v.10 By this time, one hopes that we can hear the Holy Spirit when He says: "For this reason the woman ought to have a symbol of authority on her head, *because of the angels!*" Head-covering is not for this physical world at all. It is to identify a person's spiritual position to angelic beings. It is a flag that proclaims which side we are on. There are two kinds of angels, holy and fallen, and both kinds are about us all the time. If a woman does not cover her head, she is showing her apostate or lost condition to holy angels and demons. She is giving the enemy access to attack her mind. Since a woman is "one flesh" with her husband, his spiritual condition is also being displayed.

vs.11-12 These verses show that God is no respecter of gender. Men and women are equal before the throne of grace.

v.13-15 The Lord is giving us credit for a lot more spiritual insight than we exhibit today. Here He is expecting us to understand the spiritual significance of the previous 12 verses. It is a remarkable natural phenomenon that a woman's hair will grow longer and faster than a man's hair. Since the Lord Jesus is ever present, the woman as a type of the church should continually hide her glory that the Lord might get all the glory. God gave long hair to woman as His covering and a wrap. The Greek word here is *peribolaion* (Strong's No.4018g, which may be defined as "that which is thrown around"). The point being, that a *katakalupto_* is not a *peribolaion.* It appears that hair was given as a natural wrap to all women on earth, but that wrap does not constitute a *katakalupto-*, a prayer covering, which comes down over the head. For women, heads covered or heads shaved are the only two conditions permitted, vs.5-6. We are not excused from obeying vs.5-6 and 10 by v.15! Many churches require that women be veiled during all conscious hours of the day.

V:16 This is the only verse in this whole passage which could be culturally interpreted. In the 1st century, neither Greek men nor women covered their heads as a daily practice. Jewish men and women both did. The extant pictorial records of both cultures are too conclusive for debate. That *only* women should wear a head covering was a practice *peculiar* to the church. That is probably what Paul meant when he said, "We (the Jews) have no such practice, nor have the (Gentile) churches of God." The NASB appears to translate the intent of this verse more clearly than the literal NKJV. But regardless of how we wish to interpret vs.15-16, they in no way negate the direct commands of vs.5-6 and 10. The Lord did not inspire Paul to write 12 verses on head-covering, just to do away with them in one.

Another approach to understanding v.16, is to ask: Which question is Paul answering? Looking up to verse 13, Paul asks, "Judge among yourselves. Is it proper for women to pray to God with head uncovered?" vs.14-15 are parenthetic, and Paul answers his question in v.16 with, "But if anyone seems to be contentious, we have no such custom, nor do the churches of God."

CHAPTER SIX

Hazardous Theology

Maybe we ought to look at the other side of the coin: Many churches that disregard these commands claim to have the "greater gifts" of the Holy Spirit, 1 Corinthians 12:31. But by their disobedience to these statutes, these same churches are showing to angelic majesties that they are unsaved, or are Christians in rebellion to the Bible. Gifts of the Holy Spirit and rebellion just don't go together. Would the Lord give a spiritual gift to someone in open disobedience to His written Word?

It's fine to believe that the gifts of the Spirit are for the whole Christian Era; but it is spiritual Russian roulette to ignore the commands that appear just before, and just after them. 1st Corinthians 12 is like a "gifts highway," while chapters 11 and 14 are like rules of the road. Running the wrong way down a highway can get you killed. Running the wrong way down a spiritual road can ravage your soul. 1st Corinthians 11 and 14 contain directives which regulate the exercise of the gifts. It is hazardous to ignore them.

We can't have it both ways. If the Bible is really God's Word, we can't go picking through the verses of 1st Corinthians, accepting what we like, and rejecting what we don't. If the gifts are for today, so are the commands. If the commands are only for the 1st century, so are the gifts. Remember that Satan's primary weapon is deception. Genuine spiritual warfare is a truth battle. To win this battle, we have to be intellectually honest:

> 2 Peter 3:15-16 ...as also our beloved brother Paul, according to the wisdom given to him, has written to you, as also in all his epistles, **speaking in them of these things, in which are some things hard to understand, which untaught and unstable *people* twist to their own destruction, as *they do also* the rest of the Scriptures.**

And many do distort 1st Corinthians. Here is an example as told to me by a brother who attends a large Pentecostal church:

> "In a service last August, Pastor Vebb gave us a sermon on obedience to the Bible. It sounded just great, and many people told me later how they like our church because, 'They preach straight from the Word here.' But Hurricane Andrew was on its way, and Pastor Vebb said that there was a woman in the congregation who had a prophecy for the whole church on the subject. He invited the woman up front to speak to the assembly. She prophesied something to the effect that the safest place to be was in the eye of the storm. People were saying, 'Praise the Lord, Hallelujah,' and so on; but I doubt if those devastated and homeless people in Homestead, Florida would have bought her idea."

Sounded great, but it was a false prophecy. Simple to recognize without waiting to see if it came true: the submission ordinance was not obeyed. The above "prophetess" did not have her head covered when she prophesied, so the minute she opened her mouth to speak, she was in disobedience to God's command to cover her head when prophesying, 1 Corinthians 11:5-6! But all these churches can't be wrong, can they? Well take your pick. Either the churches are wrong, or the Bible is. If that prophecy were of God, the Holy Spirit empowered that woman to disobey 1 Corinthians 11:5-6, and that's impossible, Numbers 23:19.

The vast gulf which separates a false prophecy from a true one is best illustrated by contrasting the two. Listen to what Leonhard Keyser, an Anabaptist, said in August 1552, on the day of his death:

> In the second year of his ministry, Leonhard Keyser was apprehended at Scharding, in Baveria, and condemned by the Bishop of Passau, and other priests and capilaries, to be burned on Friday, before St. Lawrence Day, in August of the same year. Having bound him on a cart, they took him to the fire... When he came out into the field and was approaching the fire, he, bound as he was, leaned down at the side of the cart, and plucked a flower with his hand, saying to the judge who rode on horseback along side of the cart: "Lord judge, here I pluck a flower; if you can burn this flower, and me, you have justly condemned me; but on the other hand, if you cannot burn me and this flower in my hand, consider what you have done, and repent."
>
> Thereupon the judge and the three executioners threw an extraordinary quantity of wood into the fire, in order to burn him immediately to ashes by the great fire. But when the wood was entirely burned up, his body was taken from the fire uninjured. Then the executioners and their assistants built another great fire of wood, which when it was consumed, his body still remained uninjured, only his nails and his hair were somewhat burned brown, and, the ashes having been removed from his body, the latter was found smooth and clear, and the flower in his hand, not withered, or burned in the least.
>
> The executioners then cut his body into pieces, which they threw into a new fire. When the wood was burned up, the pieces lay unconsumed in the fire. Finally they took the pieces and threw them into the river Inn. The judge was so terrified by this occurrence that he resigned his office, and moved to another place.
>
> His chief servant, who was with the judge, and saw and heard all this, came to us in Moravia, became our brother, and lived and died piously. That it might not be forgotten, our teachers have recorded this as it came from his own lips, and now cause it to be promulgated and made known.[45]

---

45 Thieleman J. van Braght, *Martyrs Mirror*, (Scottdale, PA, Herald Press, 1950) pp420-421.

The major requirement of a prophecy from God, is that it comes true. Leonhard Keyser's did, that woman's didn't. But more was amiss in that Pentecostal church during that Sunday service than just a "little" false prophecy. The pastor himself invited his "prophetess" to disobey the following commands:

> 1 Corinthians 14:34-40 (excerpts) **Let your women keep silent in the churches, for they are not permitted to speak;** but *they are* to be submissive, as the law also says... **for it is shameful for women to speak in church.**

> 1 Timothy 2:11-12 **Let a woman learn in silence with all submission. And I do not permit a woman to teach or to have authority over a man, but to be in silence.**

So much for his sermon on obedience. Teaching one way while walking another. "But, big deal," you say, "Whom did she hurt? Nothing bad seems to have happened to anyone; and besides, that's only three minor statutes in a couple of Pauline epistles".[46]

Maybe, but speaking falsely in the name of the Lord is no light thing. In the Old Testament, they stoned you for it. He who is "above every name that is named, both now and in the age to come" is an absolutely Holy God, who dwells in unapproachable light. In Him there is no shadow of turning. Why aren't these people terrified? I sure would be. These assemblies are practicing exactly what got Moses, Nadab and Abihu, Korah, and the elders of Israel killed: worshiping in a false spirit... seizing authority... breaking types... Are such things pleasing in the sight of the Lord of Sabaoth, Jehovah of Hosts?

---

46 That a woman may pray and prophesy is obvious from 1 Corinthians 11:5-6. She may do so, of course, any time it does not break a type of Christ; i.e., any time a Christian man is not present in the gathering. Since Scripture mandates that a woman cover her head only when "praying or prophesying," if she cannot pray or prophesy with men present, why should she cover her head in church? 1 Corinthians 11:10 states "because of the angels" and, as a type of the church, v.15, to hide her glory in the presence of the Lord. When in church, women silently pray as do all. When is there a better time to display this sign than when we assemble? This is not to imply that women should wear a head-covering during church only.

> 1 Peter 1:17 And if you call on the Father, who without partiality judges according to each one's work, conduct yourselves throughout the time of your stay *here* in fear;

It is one thing to *talk* about obedience; it is something else to *be* obedient! Many today are deceived by the sound of sanctity, while the reality thereof is far off. Many even say that these commands were addressed to an unruly 1st Century Corinthian church, but that is not what the Bible says. 1 Corinthians 1:2 reads, **"...with all who in every place call on the name of Jesus Christ our Lord..."** If that address includes you, then those commands are to you. Not only that, but these principles were taught in every church:

> 1 Corinthians 4:17 ...as I teach every where **in every church.**

Now, notice that the "submissiveness" quote above is from the pastoral epistle to Timothy. Timothy was in Ephesus, 1 Timothy 1:31 Any contention that these laws were addressed to an unruly 1st Century Corinthian church is just not true. There is no hint from the sublime epistle to the Ephesians that the Ephesians were unruly, or an assembly in disregard of authority.[47] Woman's silence of I Corinthians 14:34-35 is affirmed, and to that is added that a woman should not teach or hold authority over a man, which reinforces Genesis 3:16. Genesis 3:16 is part of creation law, and as such, is applicable to all mankind regardless of the time period in which we may be.

Satan Tempted Eve

So what is this all about? Why were these commands given? Everything from creation on to our own time (including the types) was designed to bring glory to the Lord Jesus, Colossians 1:16. If our spiritual eyes are open, we see typologically that the church should receive instruction from the Lord with quiet submissiveness. Certainly the church cannot teach or hold authority over the Son of God, 1 Timothy 2:11-12.

---

47 This letter to Timothy at Ephesus was written later than Paul's epistle to the Ephesians. It is probable that 1 Timothy 2:8-15 represents the practical applications of the type of Christ and the Church which Paul had already outlined in his earlier epistle to that church. See Ephesians 5:21-88.

> 1 Timothy 2: 13-14 For Adam was formed first, then Eve. And Adam was not deceived, but the woman being deceived, fell into transgression.

In v.13: "Adam was created first," affirms God's governmental order. In v.14: "the woman being quite deceived" amplifies the reason for it, and is most important. It brings to our attention a strange phenomenon of man's nature. It appears that women are more sensitive to messages from spirits than men are. They have better spiritual antennae, I suppose. This is easily provable today. Mediums, fortunetellers, palmists and witches are rarely men.

That is why Satan tempted Eve... she could get the message! When the first woman turned to a message from a spirit, and shared it with her husband, it caused the fall of man. The Lord is reminding us of the fall here, and telling men not to listen to women who are listening to spirits... that it is not in our best interest to do so. Can we hear that? Not a chance! Our sisters' minds are filled with escaping male domination and breaking cultural molds.

Despite these warnings in the Bible, some women are again receiving messages from the spirits. About 90% of these "tongues" are uttered by women, and men of the church are listening. The first time, it led to the fall of man... this time it will probably lead to the fall of the church, the great apostasy. Impossible? Wait until you read the rest of this book before you say so.[48] A dear pastor's wife in the midwest expressed the scriptural viewpoint when she wrote:

> After a few disastrous attempts to spiritually "guide" my husband, I quickly learned how susceptible I myself was to being led astray, or to taking over the "headship" role. Now, when I feel some spiritual revelation coming on, I pray, "Lord, if I am hearing from You, then show/change my husband. If I am not hearing from You, then show/change me." I continue to diligently study the Word, and pray that prayer, until the Lord brings about a change either in my husband or me.

---

48 The author has been criticized for homing in on the demonic spiritual phenomena that are currently being exhibited within the churches. But this book is not intended as a balanced doctrinal exegesis of the gifts of the Holy Spirit. Instead, its goal is to present scriptural methods of unmasking and fighting against the kingdom of darkness.

Dear Christian wives, be very, very careful when you discuss spiritual matters with your husbands. Be careful, because of your wonderful, God-given, but spiritually dangerous sensitivity. You could lead the man you love astray.

Husbands and Wives

The following quotes contain no specific rules which may be typologically interpreted; nonetheless, they are tender little spiritual glimpses of the beauty and the witness of the church as the Lord would desire to see it. All Christians should be able to see themselves mirrored here:

> Titus 2:3-11 ...the older women likewise, that they be reverent in behavior, not slanderers, not given to much wine, teachers of good things – that they admonish the young women to love their husbands, to love their children, to *be* discrete, chaste, homemakers, good, obedient to their own husbands, that the word of God may not be blasphemed.
>
> Likewise exhort the young men to be sober-minded, in all things showing yourself *to be* a pattern of good works; in doctrine *showing* integrity, reverence, incorruptibility, sound speech that cannot be condemned, that one who is an opponent may be ashamed, having nothing evil to say of you.
>
> *Exhort* bondservants to be obedient to their own masters, to be well-pleasing in all *things*, not answering back, not pilfering, but showing all good fidelity, that they may adorn the doctrine of God our Savior in all things. For the grace of God that brings salvation has appeared to all men,...

What a blessing these verses are when we look at them as the type of the church. We can see what the Lord desires the witness of the saints to be before the world, and the angelic hosts. The type of Christ and the church is again alluded to in "that the word of God may not be dishonored."

A typological, word-by-word exegesis of the following passage could take a whole chapter (not appropriate here), but it is a wonderful subject for personal devotions:

> 1 Peter 3:1-4 Wives, likewise, *be* submissive to your own husbands, that even if some do not obey the word, they, without a word, may be

won by the conduct of their wives, when they observe your chaste conduct *accompanied* by fear. Do not let your adornment be [merely]* outward – arranging the hair, wearing gold, or putting on *fine* apparel – rather *let it be* the hidden person of the heart, with the incorruptible *beauty* of a gentle and quiet spirit, which is very precious in the sight of God. ***(Note, 2nd edition: the word [merely] above, is not in the original Greek, demonstrating the unreliable nature of the NKJV, and many other modern Bible translations).**

1 Peter 3:5-6 For in this manner, in former times, the holy women who trusted in God also adorned themselves, being submissive to their own husbands, as Sarah obeyed Abraham, calling him lord, whose daughters you are if you do good and are not afraid with any terror.

It needs to be said right here, and will be repeated again. None of these verses teaches male superiority.[49] To believe that they do, is one of the "doctrines of demons," part of the deception of the enemy. Satan will use any lie he can to lead us into rebellion. Remember that women (as a type of the church) have the sacred duty of showing the spiritual condition of the church to all creation. This chain of command is not about male chauvinism; it's about God's government. Satan rebelled against God's governmental order, and today he is getting the church to do the same thing under the guise of equality for women. The Bible states that men and women are equal before the Lord, but this equality does not give us license to disregard God's chain of command.

Let's look at a little earthly example: Is the governor of the state, or the local policeman, any "better" than anyone else in God's eyes? Of course not. They are men for whom Christ died, just like the rest of us. Nevertheless, they represent an earthly authority which we dare not disobey. If we openly rebel against them, we can go to jail or get killed. God has not "given them the sword for nothing," Romans 13:4. If we respect man's governmental authority out of fear, what should our attitude be toward God's governmental order for the saints?

On earth, when governments become brutal or repressive, history shows that rebellion is soon to follow: The American Revolution is an example. God's government is never repressive, of course, but His delegated representatives can sometimes be. If husbands are unkind or coercive, they should not be surprised by the rebellion of their wives. Husbands, be in fear if your wife submits to you because of the law of

49 1 Corinthians 11:11-12 and Galatians 3:28 make that quite clear.

God while you are abusive or immoral. If she is obedient while you rebel. Here is why. If we have a Righteous King and a righteous servant, and in between there is a steward who mistreats that King's servant, it will not be long before the Righteous King punishes the unjust steward. That is the way good government works, and the Lord's government is perfect:

- Matthew 24:48-51 "But if that evil servant says in his heart, 'My master is delaying his coming,' and begins to beat *his* fellow servants, and to eat and drink with the drunkards, the master of that servant will come on a day when he is not looking for *him* and at an hour that he is not aware of, and will cut him in two and appoint *him* his portion with the hypocrites. There shall be weeping and gnashing of teeth.

Wife, pray for your husband if he mistreats you; please forgive him, and fear for him. The Lord has not forgotten you, and sooner or later God's disciplining hand will rest heavily upon that man. He has broken a type of Christ. Jesus never oppresses the church.

These are not new truths. They have been with us for millennia. But what our fathers knew and taught in the church is hidden from us now. Until a generation ago, the submission ordinance was understood and observed the world over. In some countries (where the church is persecuted) it is still being observed, thus fulfilling 2 Timothy 3:12, "All those who desire to live Godly in Jesus Christ *shall* be persecuted." Persecution accompanies standing for the Lord today, just as it always has.

It is interesting to note that the explosion of the world-wide charismatic experience did not enter the church until after these precepts were generally disregarded. If that means what it appears to mean, it would be to our advantage to get our spiritual heads screwed back on straight, and our doctrines and behavior back in line with what the Bible directs. In our rushing headlong after each new spiritual experience and phenomenon, we have forgotten to check with our guidebook, the Word of God. We need to ask what has caused us to become so lax that we allow all forms of worldliness in our own lives, and in the church. Why have we permitted our children to become addicted to rock music, drugs or satanism? What is the relationship between the ordinance we are ignoring and the falling away of the church?

CHAPTER SEVEN

Spirits In My house

Conservative Christians today hear many arguments about the evils of false gifts, but no matter how well this evidence is presented, somehow it lacks the convicting power of the Holy Spirit. Why? Because most of the men who write those critiques neither teach, nor obey, the submission ordinance or the associated commands. So how can those who interpret away part of the Bible expect the Holy Spirit to empower what they say? No obedience means no power! Strange as it may seem, there appears to be a relationship between head-covering and true spiritual insight. Numerous saints report that after the submission ordinance is observed, most gross heresies become clearly obvious to them. Here is the account of one family who decided to obey the Word, and to whom error became immediately evident:

> "We are Pentecostals, but someone gave us a copy of *Sunset of the Western Church* anyway. We were not sure it was right; but we really love the Lord, so my wife started covering her head. On the following Sunday, while the pastor was preaching, I became aware that there was a demon standing right behind him. I am a business man, not a dreamer, so this came as quite a shock. I had never sensed anything like that before in my life.
>
> So we left that church, and went to another Assembly of the same denomination. During one part of the service, many in this Assembly started praying in tongues. I was instantly aware that the air above us was filled with evil spirits. I was very frightened and upset, and looked over to make sure my wife's head was covered.

> After the service, we waited outside to talk to the pastor. I opened the Bible, and the pastor suddenly said to me, 'Have you come to trouble us?' I heard that spirit! It sounded so close to what the demoniac of Gergesenes said to Jesus that we left that church, and have not been back since.[50]
>
> I know the gift of discernment of spirits is biblical; but I fear it, and am afraid of being deceived. So I always command this spirit to confess Jesus (1 John 4:1-3), which He does. But having this ability is a very humbling thing, and I don't tell very many people about it."

Demons are in the church, and a few brothers with the rare gift of discernment are aware of them. Many charismatics claim to have this gift, but I know of no one without a head-covering wife who really does. In fact, most of the families where head-covering is observed for the first time, declare that they either have a better understanding of the Word, or a new sensitivity to false doctrine. Others have become aware of demonic influences around them, as was true for this brother in north Florida:

> I was a deacon at the 1st Baptist Church of__, Florida. I read your *Sunset of the Western Church,* and asked my wife to please start covering her head, which she did. A couple of Sundays later I tried to give a copy of *Sunset* to one of my best friends, a fellow deacon. He refused to take it. So I offered the book to his wife.
>
> She refused to touch it, and said, 'That's bondage!' My jaw dropped. To my knowledge, neither of them had ever seen the book before. I looked up at the woman's face, and saw a gray halo around her head. So then I understood what kind of spirit would be in bondage if she obeyed God's Word.
>
> Shortly after that, I sensed that there were evil spirits in my house. I saw them as gray shadows in the comers of some of the rooms. I commanded all the evil spirits to leave in Jesus' name, and have not been aware of any around here for quite some time now.

In the name of Jesus, that deacon commanded the evil spirits to leave, and they did. Where did his authorization to do this come from? Remember when we were saved, how the Holy Spirit opened the Word to us, so that each day new spiritual truths just seemed to pop

50 Matthew 8:29 And suddenly they cried out, saying, "What have we to do with You, Jesus, You Son of God? *Have You come here to torment us before the time?"*

off the pages of the Bible? When we come under the submission ordinance, the same wonderful thing happens. We walk up another step on the staircase of our Christian growth. Suddenly, passages of Scripture which were obscure to us become clear as a mountain stream. Verses such as:

> Matthew 18:18 ...whatever you bind on earth will be bound in Heaven,

> John 20:23 If you forgive the sins of any, they are forgiven them; if you retain the *sins* of any, they are retained.

We learn that these verses can become true in our lives, that we rule with Christ, as Scripture says, not in abstract theory, but in actuality, over a real spiritual kingdom that exists today![51] We learn about spiritual authority...what it is, and how the Lord delegates it. We learn that the Lord does not give spiritual authority to anyone who is not totally submitted to His will, any more than an earthly government would give a nuclear sub to a rebel (the weapons that would be under his control are far too dangerous). It is also far too dangerous to give spiritual authority to anyone unless it is the Lord, and *only* the Lord who is calling the shots. Here is an example of real spiritual authority as quoted from the records of the Anabaptists:

> In AD 1556, or thereabouts, there was in Beverwijk, Holland, a brother named Augustine, a baker by trade, who had forsaken the world, and been baptized upon his faith, according to the ordinance of Christ, which the papists could not endure. There was at that time a burgomaster who was very bitter, and filled with perverted zeal, who sometimes said that he would furnish the peat and wood to burn Augustine. The bailiff had said that he should not apprehend Augustine without previously warning him; but he did not keep his word, for he came upon a time when Augustine was at his work, kneading dough. Perceiving him, Augustine attempted to flee, but was instantly seized by his pursuers, and cast into prison.
>
> As he was a man who was much beloved, it greatly grieved the bailiff's wife, who said to her husband: "O you murderer, what have you done!" but all in vain, he had to follow his Lord Jesus as a lamb is led to the slaughter. As he steadfastly adhered to his faith, they passed a cruel sentence on him, namely that he should be tied to a ladder, and thus

51 1 Peter 2:5-9, Revelation 1:6, 5:10.

cast alive into the fire, and burnt.

On his way to death, he saw one of his acquaintances, to whom he said: "Farewell, Joost Cornelissen."

The latter, prompted by his good opinion of him, replied in a friendly manner: "I hope that we shall hereafter be together forever."

Whereupon said burgomaster replied out of a heart judging with partiality: "He will not get to the place whither you will go; but he goes from this fire to the eternal."

Thereupon Augustine said to the burgomaster: "I cite you to appear within three days before the judgment seat of God."

As soon as the execution was over, the burgomaster was instantly smitten with a raging sickness, and continually cried with a guilty conscience: "Peat and wood, peat and wood!" so that it was terrible to hear; and before the three days had expired, he died; which was a great sign of the all-seeing eye of God, who would not suffer such cruelty to go unpunished, as an example to all those who from perverse blindness should commit such deeds.[52]

Awesome. The hand of God. By the Word of the Lord, as spoken through His servant Augustine, that Burgomaster was condemned to death. Who could display such power while walking in the flesh? Brother Augustine passed the scriptural test of the true prophet:

Deuteronomy 18:22 ...when a prophet speaks in the name of the LORD, if the thing does not happen or come to pass... The prophet has spoken it presumptuously; you shall not be afraid of him.

A vast gulf separates the true from the counterfeit. Look at the difference between the judgment on that Burgomaster, and the so-called spiritual gifts seen today. Augustine was 100% accurate, and the Lord got the glory. Augustine the baker was not some puffed-up egocentric crowing about his "anointing." He wasn't some wild-eyed ecstatic, writhing on the floor, while muttering in some kind of unintelligible secret language, Isaiah 8:19-20. A ludicrous comparison. When the God of Heaven shows His power, mountains tremble.

The Lord performs miracles every day. It's a miracle when a heart is changed. Miraculous 'coincidences," including the appearance of angels, have been recorded throughout the Christian Era. But the Lord's spiritual power is not usually exhibited today by notable

---

52 Thieleman J. van Braght, *Martyrs Mirror* (Scottdale, PA: Herald Press 1950), p553

miracles such as the one cited above. The author has not found more that a dozen or so verifiable spectacular miracles (recorded by reputable Christian historians) which have taken place during the whole Christian Era. Instead, as Scripture declares, we see God's power through the "foolishness of preaching," as spoken by some humble man of God... usually followed by a quickening of the Holy Spirit, which leads the lost to Jesus or a church to repentance.

True Authority

God's Word is the authority, and Christians are commanded to submit to it, and almost as important, to "submitting to one another in the fear of God," Ephesians 5:21. This also goes for pastors, priests, teachers, elders, and deacons. No one is above these rules. God does indeed set offices in the church, but not to "lord it over the brethren," 1 Peter 5:3. All Christians are equal before the Throne of Grace. If the least member of the body perceives a truth from God's Word, all must submit to that truth. Again, the Word is the authority. If a brother needs to be corrected or disciplined, it is the authority of God through His Word that must do so. Moses knew this, and did not correct Korah himself, Numbers 16. He let God do so. Moses understood that he had no authority within himself. The only time he exhibited his own authority was when he struck the rock twice, an act he lived to regret, Deuteronomy 32:48-52.

When a servant of God quotes the Word, he is speaking with absolute authority. His authority is diminished by whatever degree he dilutes God's Words with his own. True spiritual authority is a litmus test of our willingness to make Jesus the Lord of our life, and it cannot be separated from a servant's humility. Moses probably had more spiritual authority imputed to him by God than any other man who ever lived (except Jesus). He was also the meekest, Numbers 12:3. If we lack spiritual power in our Christian service, it is because we are not totally broken before the Lord.

True spiritual authority is delegated in direct proportion to our submission, and visible to all through our walk. God's servants are obedient to the Bible. The more submitted a true servant of the Lord becomes, the less willing he is to depart from scriptural truth, and the more he fears to presumptuously exceed his authority:

> Deuteronomy 18:20 'But the prophet, who shall presume to speak a word in My name, which I have not commanded him to speak... that prophet shall die.'

Today, there are charismatic churches that encourage people to speak prophetically; trusting, I suppose, that the Lord would give someone a prophecy upon request. God's true prophets did. not prophesy because they "sought the gift," but because God commanded them to prophesy, Amos 7:15, and they were unfailingly, 100% accurate. There is a whole gaggle of inaccurate "prophets" in Kansas City who claim divine inspiration, but the account of the 400 friends of Zedekiah the son of Chenaanah (2 Chronicles 18:8-27) and others, would lead us to believe otherwise. The biblical test for a true prophet is his 100% accuracy, Deuteronomy 18:22. The Kansas City seers "prophesy" correctly only a little better that half the time (60% or thereabouts), so they fail God's 100% test.[53] The Bible itself shows them to be false prophets, and it's no light thing to speak in the name of the Lord, when the Lord has not spoken:

> Jeremiah 28:15-17 Then the prophet Jeremiah said to Hananiah the prophet, "Hear now, Hananiah, the LORD has not sent you, but you make this people trust in a lie." Therefore thus says the LORD: "Behold, I will cast you from the face of the earth. This year you shall die, because you have taught rebellion against the Lord." So Hananiah the prophet died the same year in the seventh month.

God will not grant spiritual authority, nor place His stamp of approval on anyone who is not in submission to His Word. If power is being displayed by someone in open disobedience to the Bible, the power he is wielding is *not* the Lord's power.[54] It is the enemy's, through violent men attempting to "take the kingdom of God by force," Matthew 11:12. The church is overrun with these aggressive and willful seekers of power, these latter-day Korahs, Numbers 16:1-35.

Spiritual authority is really God's own authority that He delegates to His servant. Christians are God's messengers to the world, and true messengers do not tarnish the pure message of the Gospel with agendas of their own. Nor do they place personal experiences or feelings above the inspired Scripture.

---

53 John McArthur, *Charismatic Chaos,* (Grand Rapids, Zondervan 1992) pp67-68.

54 Joshua 7:11, Isaiah 14:18-15, 16:14, John 1, Numbers 16.

Holy Angels, Fallen Angels

Those are the rules, here is the application: During our lives here on earth, we are constantly surrounded by unseen spirit beings. Which kind we relate to, and how we interact with them is determined for us by Scripture. There are holy angels and fallen angels. God's angels protect us from demonic attack, Psalm 91:11, Judges 9. When we obey "Let a woman have a symbol of authority on her head," 1 Corinthians 11:10, we do so **"BECAUSE, OF THE ANGELS."** Can the fallen angels be prevented from attacking us, or can the holy angels legally continue to protect us if we ignore this ordinance? Of course, is our initial response, but let's look at what the Bible says in the same context:

these are holy angels, not fallen angels

1 Corinthians 14:37-38 If anyone thinks himself to be prophet or spiritual, let him acknowledge that the things which I write to you are the commandments of the Lord. But if anyone is ignorant, let him be ignorant.

That is sobering. Not recognized by whom? Context implies that we will be unrecognized by Him who gave the command… that is the Lord! Consequently, this would include our guardian angels, because we are not showing *to them* that we are under the headship of Christ. This is the law as the angels see it, and Christ either confesses us before the angels, or He does not.[55] Read 1 Corinthians 11:10 and 1 Corinthians 14:37-38 again and again, until the Holy Spirit makes those verses real to your heart. Difficult as it may be to accept, "let him be ignorant" (as the NKJV translates 1 Corinthians 14:38) appears to state that the Lord will ignore our prayers if we disdain His ordinances! It is one thing to be ignorant of Scripture, it is something else to disobey it openly:

Numbers 15:30-31 But the person who does *anything* presumptuously, *whether he is* native-born or a stranger, that one brings reproach on the LORD, and he shall be cut off from among his people. Because he has despised the word of the LORD and has broken His commandment, that person shall be completely cut off; his guilt *shall be* upon him.

---

55 Luke 12:8-9 And I say to you, everyone who confesses Me before men, the Son of Man shall confess him also before the angels of God; but he who denies Me before men shall be denied before the angels of God.

Satan has deceived us into believing that a little bending of God's Word is OK, as long as everyone else is doing it. We all use "Well, there isn't any perfect church," as an excuse for accepting disobedience, or a lie.

But really look at where we are now! If we take our eyes off Satan's toys long enough to look around at the spiritual realities today, we will see that the whole world is convulsed in a titanic spiritual battle involving the awesome forces of principalities and powers in heavenly places. Satan's time is short, and he has gone forth with great fury to destroy, Revelation 12:12-17. If we allow ourselves to come out from under the protection of the forces of God, we find ourselves spiritually undefended right in the middle of the enemy's spiritual field of fire. Only one angel, "the Destroyer" of Exodus 12:23, slew all the first-born of Egypt. What human can stand before that kind of malevolent power without holy angelic help? This is of extreme gravity. What has the Lord directed Christians to do to protect themselves from this possibility?

We, too, must show spiritually that we are behind the blood on the doorposts, Exodus 12:7-13. We too must display that we are behind the Lord's protecting hand. We dare not go out. This is no game. Jackie of St. Petersburg tells of some things that happened at her house:

> Thank you for baptizing my sister and me, and teaching my whole family about the covering. A few days after I started covering my head, I began to hear loud moaning sounds coming out of our bathroom. They seemed to be coming right out of the air, about as high as my head. The lights in the room would flash on and off, and the doorknobs rattled. This happened several nights in a row. It scared my husband so bad, he called the police; but they couldn't find anything. We just bought the house, and didn't know who owned it before us. But I knew if the earlier owners were doing the occult or satanism, that things like this could happen.
>
> Somehow, I was not afraid at all. I went around to every room, and told the demons to leave in Jesus' name. I did the same thing around the yard. Then I anointed the lintels and sides of the windows and doors in the name of the Father, the Son, and the Holy Spirit. All that stuff stopped right away.

Most Christians are unaware of these demonic presences. No spiritual insight. The enemy would much rather have you believe that he's not there, to conceal his attempts to influence your mind. The "I don't really exist," lie is part of his deception. He wants you to think that the besetting sin which haunts your mind all the time is your own idea. We buy the lie, go off into sin; and the enemy wins a bout. A saint walking in sin is just another human he has fooled. Just another spiritual incompetent, he has gotten out of the fight. If we get into the spiritual battle by doing what the Bible says, demons sometimes make their disapproval known, and try to frighten the saints. Jackie was walking in the Lord, and trusted in the Lord Jesus to help her. She took a page from the Old Testament; concluding that if Passover, and anointing a house for leprosy were effectual for the Israelites, then maybe, anointing her house symbolically, would be effective for her. It appears to have been So.[56] A demonic presence was not evident to Jackie until after she covered her head, so it appears that head-covering stirs things up a bit in the enemy's camp.

This is not an unusual report. After she covered her head, Phoebe McGuire of North Dakota said that plaques and things were flying off the wall in her house; and after covering her head, Joan Donel saw demons in a church she attended. Head-covering doesn't need the approval of your pastor, or your elders, or Bible study group to work, and you're not likely to get it. But who cares? It is effective regardless of man's opinions.[57] Roy Dourine who attended a Bible study where head covering was being taught remembers a little spiritual battle:

> Despite the teacher's best efforts, the Bible study was in disorder, with women angrily denouncing head-covering and heatedly trying to discredit the Scripture on the subject. I sat quietly as long as I could, and then stood and said, "Well, I wasn't sure that what the brother was teaching was right, but now that I see the fight the devil is putting up against it, there isn't any question that it's right!"

---

56 Exodus 12:23, Leviticus 14:48-54

57 Only a few of the new head-covering sisters who have written tell of supernatural phenomena like the above. However, all tell of rich spiritual blessings which have followed their obedience to this ordinance. Some dysfunctional families have been healed. Conflicts and stresses have lessened, and lost relatives have come to the Lord.

When a woman wears a head-covering, and is silent in the church, she, as a type of the church, Ephesians 5:32, is showing to angelic majesties the *salvation of her soul,* and the church in submission to the Lord Jesus, 1 Corinthians 11:10. If she does not cover her head, speaks out in church, or teaches or holds authority over a man, 1 Timothy 2:11-12, she is showing those same angelic majesties that the church is in rebellion to the Lord. We have come out from behind our invulnerable armor. That may not frighten some, but it scares me to death.

A woman may not teach a man, not for any shallow chauvinistic or cultural reason, but because the church is subject to God the Father, through His Son; and the church has neither the knowledge nor the authority to teach anything to the Lord Jesus. If a woman teaches a man, it symbolically shows that the church can teach the Lord. Ridiculous!

A wife is submitted to her husband, not because he is any better than she is (as Scripture plainly states), but to show that the church is under the headship of Christ. Not to do so, shows the church to be in rebellion against the Lord. Thus the sin of Korah and associates is repeated.[58]

Since we are "an example unto all creation," rest assured that the fallen angels have their eyes on the church. They are aware of the spiritual significance of these things, and take advantage of the commands we disregard. Ignoring God's government opens the doors of the church to demonic attack. We have given them access by our disobedience. Head-covering is an archaic idea, but so are baptism and communion. All are 2,000 years old... the age of the church. If we wish to abandon the submission ordinance on the basis of antiquity (or the culture of the 1st century church) where shall we stop: idolatry, adultery? Those laws are older by 1,400 more years, and creation law is older still, Genesis 3:15-16.

This book is about obedience to truth. The covering just happens to be the truth which exposes the true spiritual condition of the church to all creation. By the lack of a covering, all can SEE that the church is in rebellion to the Lord.[59] This spiritual condition is visible to the evil

58 1 Corinthians 11:11-12, Galatians 3:28 and Numbers 16:1-35

59 Revelation 3:15-17, 1 John 2:15-16.

spirits, too, and they have attacked us forthwith. Note the order of events; charismatic phenomena appear after a church becomes worldly, as a bishop of a very conservative denomination reports:

> "Occasionally, we too have a church which turns liberal. The steps to separating from us go something like this: The first thing which disappears is the veiling (their word for head-covering). Next, the church becomes materialistic, and the women start wearing worldly clothes. Jewelry and makeup soon follow. After a while, they start having family problems, with divorces and re-marriages; and later some of them start speaking in tongues"[60]

It is in keeping with the holiness of God to "Spirit fill" and give out gifts *before* the church becomes like the world, not after. Real spiritual authority is delegated to God's servants most submitted to Him; yet those churches that claim the authority to exhibit the gifts of the Spirit, are the churches that refuse to obey the commands that show to the fallen angels that they are submitted to Jesus. The least submitted churches are claiming the most authority! There just has to be something wrong with that picture. If God were to honor a church's disobedience, He would cease to be holy.

Simple little things, head-covering and silence, but try to get women to obey them. They will not! Let's say that again...they will not! Why? Because the spirit of rebellion by which the church is being influenced will not let them. If you think that is a joke, or some kind of a ritualistic fable... you try. Try it with your wife, try it on your church. That is what that young pastor at Bull Creek Church tried to do. Scripture is plain, and regardless of the 17 excuses, if we believe the Bible to be the Word of God, doctrine cannot be the problem. The church is in open rebellion to the Lord, and is displaying that condition to the fallen angels.

Only if the Christian husband has the spiritual authority of the Lord through his personal submission to the Word, only if his wife sees this condition (his heart submissive to the headship of Jesus Christ in his own life), only then will she be willing to come under her husband's headship in this thing. Why? Because that is what this sign is all about. It is an external sign of an inner spiritual condition: the submission of the church to Jesus Christ.

Acts 2: 17-18, 19

60 (William C. McGrath, a Mennonite Bishop of Minerva, OH).

Husbands, the wives have not turned away from the Bible on their own. It has been with man's approval and consent, just like the Israelite women who worshiped the queen of heaven.

> Jeremiah 44:19 *The women also said,* "And when we burned incense to the queen of heaven and poured out drink offerings to her, did we make cakes for her, to worship her, and pour out drink offerings to her without our husbands' *permission*?"

Men have abandoned their spiritual headship of the home, and the chickens have come home to roost. Christian men today, by and large, are a weak-willed lot, not meriting the respect or submission of their wives.

Husbands: stand firm in the Lord, defending the authority of God's Word to your wives, but with gentleness and kindness, showing concern for their needs, as Abraham did with Sarah. To do so in a proper spirit shows symbolically that Christ holds His authority over the Church in love:

> 1 Peter 3:7 Husbands, likewise, dwell with *them* with understanding, giving honor to the wife, as to the weaker vessel, and as *being* heirs together of the grace of life, that your prayers may not be hindered.

Some men believe their headship of the home entitles them to lord it over their wives like some kind of feudal baron. Not so. Men are to lead their family as a shepherd leads the sheep. If men do not act as Christian husbands, in the full scriptural sense of the word, their behavior will come back to haunt them in the aversion, passive resistance, or open opposition of their wives. This is the way the Lord set up the system, and it works. Many brethren who observe these statutes can affirm it. The interaction between a Christian husband and his wife is a sign of the church's spiritual relationship to the Lord. Yet despite our disregard of these symbols; tongues, words of wisdom, and other phenomena are sweeping the church.

Proponents claim that this is the Holy Spirit combating the increased demonism and satanism in the world, but it is becoming terribly apparent that just the opposite is true. It appears that the enemy is introducing false gifts into the church, and leading the brethren down a garden path that can lead to the worship of angels and demons. Is that possible? If we do not show that we are submitted to Jesus, we give Satan access to do just that!

It is hard to determine the correct order for the next several chapters. Disobedience has led to a faulty Christian walk… Which has led to faulty doctrine... Which has led to further disobedience... Which has led to a more faulty walk... Which has led to more false doctrine... Which has led to further disobedience... And round and round we go... but from what vantage point should we view the merry-go-round that Lucifer is leading the church to ride?

CHAPTER EIGHT

Lying Spirits

Since the Word tells us that the Holy Spirit leads us into all truth, John 16:13, for the mature brethren this book could probably end right here. However, for younger Christians not yet nurtured in the Word, it might be well to amplify a few points. Right up front, the author believes the gifts of the Spirit are for the whole church age. He sees no scriptural reason to deny them. However, the author does not believe that the Holy Spirit of God will give a "greater gift" to someone who stands in open defiance to His Word. If God were to do so, He would be pouring out His richest blessings on the rebellious. There is a whole Bible full of examples to the contrary. The spiritual phenomenon in vogue with most charismatics is "tongues." By definition, the scriptural gift of tongues, 1 Corinthians 12:10, is the supernatural ability to speak in a language unknown to the speaker.

I can't speak Japanese. If I were to suddenly start speaking in Japanese, it would have to be because a spirit helped me do so. If this

1 Cor 13:1 1 Cor 14:39 Acts 2:6-11 Heard their own language
 1 Cor 14:26-31 Acts 19:4-6
1 Cor 14:1-5 Mark 16:17 (Jesus)

ability to speak Japanese were to continue, tomorrow's Japanese words would still have to come from a source other than my own mind. Why? Because I wouldn't know Japanese any better tomorrow than I do today. Since a tongue-speaker is speaking in a language unknown to him, for a "tongue" to be a genuine spiritual phenomenon, the speaker's words would have to come from a source other than his own mind. Otherwise, it's just fakery. Biblical tongues, by their very nature, require the interaction of an individual's spirit with the Holy Spirit of God. *If a spirit is not involved, it is NOT a spiritual gift!* It's just a delusion of the mind:

> Jeremiah 14:14 The prophets prophesy lies in My name...they prophesy to you a false vision, divination, a worthless thing, and the deceit of their heart.

Pentecostals do not obey the submission ordinance and associated commands, yet they believe that the Holy Spirit has given them various supernatural gifts. They further believe that they can go offinto disobedience, and continue to use their "gift." They believe that any future exercise of their gift, is unconditional. This disregards the nature of the spiritual gift itself. A spiritual phenomenon requires the interaction between a human spirit and another spirit. Ifthe charismatics have genuine God-given spiritual gifts, the Holy Spirit would first have to honor their disobedience to the submission ordinance and associated commands; then He would have to continue to empower them to speak in tongues and prophecies while they remained in rebellion to those statutes. That is most unlikely, because the Holy Spirit is first of all holy, and any disobedience is repugnant to Him. As a result, it is reasonable to conclude that the enemy is deceiving the charismatics with false "gifts" through mediumistic interactions with evil spirits. If a gift is of the Lord, it would be held by someone in complete submission to God's Word. Not only that, he would exhibit the fruit of being Spirit-filled:

> GAL 5:22-24 ...the fruit of the Spirit is love, joy, peace, longsuffering, kindness, goodness, faithfulness, gentleness, self-control. Against such there is no law. And those *who are* Christ's have crucified the flesh with its passions and desires.

But that is not what we see now. Today, there are no Joshuas or Daniels or Pauls. Instead, we see ordinary men and women invoking

Acts 8:14-17 Acts 10:44-46
Eph 5:18

spiritual powers outside of the scriptural guidelines which regulate our behavior. There is nothing wrong with an interest in the work of the Holy Spirit. Our battle is spiritual, Ephesians 5:11-12. But in some churches, this interest in spiritual phenomena borders on an obsession, and "the *seeking* for the filling" of the Holy Spirit is exceeding the zeal to know the Lord Jesus. That is counter to God's Word. Jesus said, "Come unto me" and "I am the Way." Scriptures that affirm the centrality of the Lord Jesus are numberless. Jesus is the central figure of our faith.[61]

> 1 Corinthians 2:2 For I determined not to know anything among you except Jesus Christ and Him crucified.

> Galatians 6:14 But God forbid that I should boast except in the cross of our Lord Jesus Christ, by whom the world has been crucified to me, and I to the world.

However, a falling away begins with just a tiny little error. Not a big, bad lie that everyone would recognize right away, but a little bending of the truth such as, "Let's *seek* for the filling of the Holy Spirit." Now doesn't that sound sanctified? We all want to be filled with the Holy Spirit, don't we? Of course. But I don't find anywhere in Scripture that I need to *seek* for Him. The Bible says that He is *given* to those who obey the Lord Jesus. Here are three of many verses that state this truth:

> John 14:16 "And I will pray the Father, and He will give you another Helper, that He may abide with you forever –

> Acts 5:32 "And we are His witnesses to these things; and *so* also *is* the Holy Spirit whom God has given to those who obey Him."

> Romans 5:5 Now hope does not disappoint, because the love of God has been poured out in our hearts by the Holy Spirit who was **given** to us.

Whats wrong with asking?

Pentecostals make much of Luke 11:13, insisting that it authorizes "seeking" for the Spirit. But even in that verse, Jesus declared that God the Father will "give the Holy Spirit to those who ask Him." *The Holy Spirit is given by a sovereign act of God.* Furthermore, when Jesus

61 Matthew 11:28, John 14:6

spoke of "asking" for the Holy Spirit in Luke 11:13, it was before Pentecost, before the Holy Spirit had been poured out on all believers, while the Levitical code was still in effect. Asking for the Holy Spirit is not mentioned anywhere after Jesus was glorified. Why? Because God the Father gave the Holy Spirit to Jesus, who in tum, poured the Spirit out on all the believers without request, Acts 1:33. If we lack the fullness of the Holy Spirit, it is because of sin and not because the Spirit is not fully indwelling the heart of the believer.[62] If we continue to "seek" for the Holy Spirit after we are indwelt by Him, we are displaying the sin of unbelief; in essence saying that we are not indwelt by Him, 1 Corinthians 6:19, or that we are not complete in Christ, Colossians 2:9-10. Impossible, Numbers 23:19!

The Bible states clearly that the Holy Spirit is *given* to those who obey God. Nowhere does Scripture declare that the Holy Spirit will be given to those who *seek!* Subtle... but then we are dealing with a very cunning enemy. *The Holy Spirit was not sent to lead us unto Himself, but unto the Lord Jesus!* Any leading of a spirit which takes our eyes off the Lord Jesus, *cannot* be of the Holy Spirit of God. Meditate on that a long time:

> Jesus said, "He will bear testify of Me," and "He will NOT speak on His own authority, but whatever He hears, He will speak."[63]

This is such an important point that it must be emphasized. Any spirit which influences us to take our eyes off the Lord Jesus, to worship a spirit, is not the Holy Spirit of God! That is not what the Holy Spirit came here to do. Jesus said, "He will bear witness of Me." That is a direct Bible statement.

There are many lying spirits. Why should we believe them? Would you believe me if I told you I was George Washington? Of course not. Neither should you believe the "claims" of some spirit, no matter how good he sounds, if what he says is not in accord with what Scripture states. Satan was a liar from the beginning, and now he is trying to deceive the saints into believing that he is the Holy Spirit. He looks beautiful, just as the Bible warned us he would, 2 Corinthians 11:13-15.

---

62 Acts 1:33, Romans 5:5, Ephesians 4:30, 1 Thessalonians 5:19, Titus 3:6.

63 John 10:1-5, John 14:16-17, John 14:26, 15:26, [16:13], Titus 3:5-6.

But no matter what a spirit *claims* to be, if a spirit leads people to worship a spirit, it is not the work of the Holy Spirit of God. It is a false spirit, with a false doctrine, John 16:14. Who then is that spirit? It is from the enemy. It is a demon!

Many churches today have turned their eyes from the cross unto angels and spirits, Colossians 2:18. That is not wisdom from above. Jesus is central, from the creation until the eternal kingdom of God the Father.[64] We are not directed to *seek* the Holy Spirit, but we are commanded to know Jesus.[65] However, once we swallow the little lie (that we have to *seek* for the filling of the Holy Spirit) then we can proceed to bigger and better untruths. Try this one:

It is said, "Everyone who is baptized in the Holy Spirit will have the evidence of speaking in other tongues." There is not a single verse of Scripture that says anything of the kind, and it is directly contrary to several.

> 1 Corinthians 12:7-11 But the manifestation of the Spirit **is given** to each one for the profit *of all*: for to one is given the word of wisdom through the Spirit, and **to another** the word of knowledge through the same Spirit; **to another** faith by the same Spirit, **to another** gifts of healings by the same Spirit, **to another** the working of miracles, **to another** prophecy, **to another** discerning of spirits, **to another** *different* kinds of tongues, **to another** the interpretation of tongues. But one and the same Spirit works all these things, distributing to each one individually **as He wills.**

> 1 Corinthians 12:30 Do all have gifts of healings? Do all speak with tongues? Do all interpret?

When the Bible states one thing, and we maintain something else, what do we call it: either deception or willful blindness. From the above Scriptures, it is apparent that spiritual gifts were given by God's sovereign will, and not as a result of someone's "seeking." It is also clear that different people received different gifts, while only some received tongues. To state then that all are to speak in tongues as a sign of the filling of the Spirit *is a lie of the devil!* It is directly contrary to the Word of God. It is flagrant heresy.

---

64 Matthew 28:18, Colossians 1:15-18, 2:9·10, Ephesians 1:20-23

65 Matthew 11:28, John 6:37, 12:46, 16:18-15, Acts 17:27, 1 Corinthians 2:2, Philemon 8:7-12, Revelation 8:20

Not only that, "tongues" is the wrong yardstick by which to measure the believer's spiritual condition. Jesus Himself said, "By their fruits," (not by their gifts) "you shall know them," Luke 6:44. Satan can, and has, faked the gifts, Exodus 7:9-22.[66] He is a past master at it. Anyone who believes that witchcraft, voodoo, or demon worship do not work is uninformed. A couple of years ago, we received a phone call about this sort of thing from Charles, an ex-satanist in Pennsylvania:

> "I just read *Sunset of the Western Church,* and what you said about false gifts is absolutely true! I was a warlock in a major coven here in Philadelphia. I was into demonism, the occult, black magic, the whole lot. One witch in our coven was always speaking in tongues.
>
> Somehow, the Lord saved me out of all that. I didn't know where to go to church, so I went to a local Pentecostal Assembly. Everything seemed alright until a traveling evangelist came to church. He called for all those who wanted to be filled with the Spirit to come down front. I went, but what I heard was the same identical tongue that the witch spoke in our black masses.
>
> I knew that the Holy Spirit of God would not be in both places, but a demon could be; so I left that church."

Satanic rock concerts have altar calls and healing services. Sound familiar? It should. Many churches have the same thing. But we are not commanded in Scripture to have altar calls or healing services, so the source is the same, Deuteronomy 12:32. We hold hands in a circle to pray, just as the mediums do when they call up a spirit; but the Bible does not command us to copy the rituals of the occult, 1 Timothy 2:8. If we copy the rituals of the occult, those occult spirits will gain access to the church. People who are actively engaged in occult practices recognize a "familiar spirit" right away. Sarah Barby writes:

Satan is an imposter so how do we not know that Christians didn't pray first in circles then the occult copied that. That's the same with tongues.

66 One Baptist pastor told me of a Roman Catholic to whom he had been personally witnessing. This Catholic man did not understand the plan of salvation, and had not accepted the Lord. One day he walked into a Pentecostal church. While crossing the threshold he was rendered unconscious (slain in the spirit), and when he came to, he started speaking in tongues. This account is very revealing. If the Holy Spirit of God did it, then a spiritual gift was given by God to a man who professed to be unsaved.

"When another guest at an anniversary party heard that I was interested in prophecy, he started to talk to me. What I heard was frightening. He said that ever since childhood he had been hearing voices which foretold the future. He further stated that, during college, he had even sought advice from a channeler *(translate that medium)* about future events. I told him of the terrible spiritual danger he was in, and asked if he ever went to church.

"Oh yes," he said, "I go to a charismatic church and enjoy it very much. I feel the same spiritual presence there."

"From reading *Bondage Breaker* I understood that he was being influenced by a demon, and that he was sensing the same demonic presence in that church that he had been channeling with in the occult".

Satan is the deceiver, and through his craft he is attempting to destroy the true spiritual life of the church.[67] If he can't get rid of the Bible, he will try to introduce destructive heresies. Let's look at another one. Though the examples in the next chapter do not deal with the submission ordinance directly, they do show how ignoring the authority that God has delegated to the elders of the local church can result in demonic activity.

---

67 Exodus 12:23, Revelation 9:11

CHAPTER NINE

Magic Show

There is an error floating around the church today which in effect states that we should not judge behavior and doctrines within the church. That view is directly opposed to Scripture:

1 Corinthians 5:12 **Do you not judge those who are inside?**

1 Timothy 5:20 Those who sinning **rebuke in the presence of all...**

2 Timothy 4:2 **...Convince, rebuke, exhort,** with all longsuffering and teaching.

Titus 1:9 **...by sound doctrine, both to exhort and convict those who contradict.**

Satan's "Who are you to judge?" gimmick is just another lie to keep anyone from speaking out against heresy. But if no one is willing to stand against the wicked works of the devil, his evil doctrines will remain. So what is the scriptural way to judge false teaching without being judgmental? Jesus said:

John 12:48 "He who rejects Me, and does not receive My words, has that which judges him – **the word that I have spoken will judge him in the last day.**

So individual Christians are not supposed to judge anyone, anymore than Jesus did in John 12:18. However, if Scripture is quoted, the Word of God itself will judge the error perfectly. And saints are supposed to speak out, Ezekiel 3:18. If we don't, we end up with all the wrong people holding positions of authority in the church:

> Titus 1:10-11 **For there are many insubordinate,** both idle talkers and deceivers, especially those of the circumcision, **whose mouths must be stopped who subvert whole households,** teaching things which they ought not, for the sake of dishonest gain.

Those are not just theoretical human beings we're reading about in Titus. They are real flesh and blood people; and here is what some of those people look like. Around the country today roam self-styled "Christian faith healers." They come steaming into town with flags waving, banners flying, and radios blaring the news of their arrival:

What did Jesus & his disciples show us in their walks on the earth.

"HEALING....
FROM THE HEARTS OF
BENIE AND MARYLIN"
(to coin fictitious names)

These "healers" sound so loving, so concerned, and oh so blessedly "anointed;" but the arrogance of that statement is enough to make your blood run cold. When God heals, He does so to bring glory to His Son Jesus, and not to Benie and Marylin. If the display of their mediumistic power was all these bogus healers did, it would be bad enough, but they also get up there and preach. Their messages contain such false doctrines as "I am in the god class... I have the anointing… Jesus died spiritually, and was subject to demons... He descended into Hell and was scourged by Satan…" All are outrageous blasphemies and contrary to many Scriptures. Jesus never was, and never will be subject to any demon![68] He is the Creator, the Alpha and Omega, the I AM, and He is indivisible from God the Father.

---

68 Luke 4:36, Luke 23:43, Ephesians 1:19-23, to cite a few which come readily to mind. Jesus totally defeated the devil through the cross: Hebrews 2:14 "Since then the children share in flesh and blood, He Himself likewise also partook of the same, that through death He might render powerless him who had the power of death, that is, the devil."

These so-called faith "healers" are in direct opposition to the Bible, and are like those reckless "wandering stars, for whom the black darkness is reserved," Judges 13. Though some of them claim to love Jesus, *(they use his Holy Name often enough)* if they were to perform any healings, these healings would be mediumistic and not of the Holy Spirit. I fear for their souls, and for the spiritual well-being of those they claim to heal.

So how can we know for sure, when we speak out against some doctrine or work, that we are standing against the devil, and not some true servant of the Lord? That's easy enough. The Lord does not want His sheep to be led astray, so He made discernment simple, even for very young believers.

> Matthew 7:22-23 Many will say to Me in that day, "Lord, Lord, have we not prophesied in Your name, cast out demons in Your name, and done many wonders in Your name?" And then I will declare to them, "I never knew you; depart from Me, you who practice lawlessness."

The Bible itself exposes those who are not standing in the truth. It goes like this, if a teacher or so-called Word-Faith "healer" is not in obedience to God's Word, he is "practicing lawlessness;" and those who practice lawlessness are *NOT God's servants,* even if they spout "In Jesus' name" all the way to the second corning. If we read the Bible, and put what it states above the declarations of men, Satan will have a very difficult time selling us false doctrine.[69]

Scriptural Healing

When we look at scriptural examples of healing, they all had one thing in common. Healings were secondary to the preaching ministry of the prophet or evangelist. The healing gift, and other miracles, were given as validation for a prophetic or preaching ministry. Even for the Lord Jesus, physical healings were not central; but the miracles He performed showed God the Father's approval of the witness of His Son.[70] We see no scriptural example of a healing ministry by itself, nor is there any textual support for one. Then, as now, healing is a verifying adjunct to preaching and teaching the gospel of Jesus Christ.

---

69 1 John 3:9-10, 2:4, Jeremiah 23:25-32, Matthew 5:18-19, 7:15-22, Acts 20:29-30

70 Exodus 19:9, Luke 8:50, John 10:38, Acts 8:6,16:16-34

Now look at the contrast: In Scripture there is sound doctrine, and real miracles. Today we have "healers" who teach provably demonic doctrines. Would God validate these heresies and blasphemies with genuine miracles? If He did, God would be putting His stamp of approval on the errors they teach.

Throughout church history, there have been many stunning examples of miraculous healings, and God through His Holy Spirit still performs many miraculous healings today; but the Bible is explicit about *who* gets that gift, so that no *one* person gets the glory. Note the plurals in the following quotation: Really? John 14:12-14 (Red Letters)

> James 5:14-15 Is anyone among you sick? Let him call for the elders of the church, and let them pray over him, anointing him with oil in the name of the Lord. And the prayer of faith will save the sick, and the Lord will raise him up. And if he has committed sins, he will be forgiven.

Those are our Scriptural guidelines to miraculous healings. They are so very simple that even a child can understand them. If we are sick we are to "call the elders!" If we go somewhere else for supernatural healing, we are in direct disobedience to those verses! It doesn't matter in the least, if this traveling "healer" walks on air, breathes fire, or has sparks coming out of his ears, we are still commanded to "CALL THE ELDERS!" Any way you want to look at it, these traveling medicine shows do not represent the elders of a given church; and we find no Scripture which leads us to believe that the Lord would either add to, or circumvent, the authority He has granted to His elders to heal the sick. After all, if the Lord wills to heal us supernaturally, how many ways do we need to have available? Here is how obeying those Scriptures changed the life of Bob Hughes of Fort Myers, FL:

> My mother heard that a high percentage of 1930s blue babies (who had radiation treatment to shrink the thymus gland) later developed thyroid cancer. So in 1979, she encouraged me to have a check-up.
>
> I went to our family physician, Dr. Jack O'Brian, who ordered a thyroid scan. They found a cold nodule on my thyroid gland, and I was referred to M. D. Anderson Cancer Research Clinic in Houston, TX. At M. D. Anderson, they Xrayed my chest. From those pictures, Dr. Copeland saw that the many tumors in my lungs were inoperable.
>
> During the operation on my throat, he found mixed thyroid cancer covering my larynx, which had spread to my parotid gland and lymph glands. He took what he could, but decided to leave my voice box,

because my condition was terminal; and at best, I would live 6 months. Then I was sent home to get my affairs in order. I had completely given up, and was ready to meet my maker.

However, there is a God in heaven! I met with some church elders and Christian friends at a prayer breakfast. They laid hands on me, and prayed for my healing. I turned everything over to God, and closed the prayer by saying, "God, may Thy will be done." A few days later, I was anointed with oil.

Soon after that, Dr. Bill Kyle heard me coughing, and thought that I had also developed pneumonia. He called me into his office for new X-rays. These showed that I had a healthy set of lungs. The tumors were gone! I went to see Dr. Samaan, my endocrinologist at M. D. Anderson. He didn't believe the results of the Fort Myers Xrays, and said, "Impossible, get up to radiology. We'll shoot a new set of pictures." They too, showed that the cancer had gone. I said, "Dr. Samaan, Christ has healed me. I'll give M. D. Anderson 5% of the credit, and Jesus Christ 95%." To which Dr. Samaan replied, "Bob, in this case, you are giving us too much credit."

That is not a story which we heard from someone in East Egypt, about some nameless guy who lived in Terra del Fuego. That is a real account, about a real person, with a real address and telephone number; and Bob Hughes is alive and well in Fort Myers, FL to this very day. To the Lord Jesus, the Great Physician, goes the glory.

The Lord heals just the way he said He would, through the elders. God would never send some spectacular "anointed" healer around to lead you to disobey His command to "call the elders," any more that He would lead you into any other sin, James 1:13. Church history bears this out. Study the multitudes of healings that took place through the elders of Charles Haddon Spurgeon's church, in London, in the late 19th century. Those elders later stopped healing, because they feared that they were beginning to get the credit, rather than the Lord Jesus. It's not some big NAME up in lights, but the many little elders of the local churches who have been granted the authority to heal. Even the smallest church has elders, and in that way God gets the glory, because it is not some "anointed" man, but the Lord Himself who is the great physician.

There are other examples of the Lord's healing power that we should note. In the 19th Century, circuit pastors routinely laid hands on, and prayed for the sick. Many were healed. Just this month, a woman in Mississippi was healed of cancer after the elders of a little

Baptist church laid hands on her. At the direction of the Lord, missionaries on foreign fields have laid hands on the sick, anointing them with oil, and they have been healed. One missionary, whom the author personally knows, laid hands on a deaf man who then started to hear. Then a withered little Macedonian boy was healed. There was no church in the area, so this missionary was acting as an apostle, as "one sent" into a foreign land. He was an elder of THE church of Jesus Christ, and God's ambassador to a needy people.

Snake Oil Salesmen

There is an immense separation between the genuine work of the Holy Spirit and the healing cults. Despite the commands of Scripture, people don't go to their elders anymore. They go instead to someone with a special "anointing." Hundreds in their wheelchairs waited in line before Kathryn Kuhlman. Hundreds more with terminal cancer, gallstones, and advanced heart disease, or the like, stood before Hinn, Roberts, Ainsley, Hickey and the rest. But to date, qualified witnesses state that not one of these wizards has provided solid evidence of a single *bona fide* healing of a serious physiological disease, to any trained investigator. Not one! Nevertheless, advertising works; and critically ill people, desperately hoping for a cure, go to these performers anyway. In the euphoria of the moment, some sufferers, thinking they were cured, have even thrown their whole life's savings into the offering plate. But after returning home, they find that the root cause of their affliction remains. Case histories bear this out. In his book about the charismatic healers, Dr. William Nolen, M.D. writes:

> ...you will find no documented cures by healers of gallstones, heart disease, cancer or any other serious organic disease... **when you track the patient down to find out what happened later, you always find the "cure" to be purely symptomatic and transient. The underlying disease remains.**[71]

This is just one example of the mountain of evidence that contradicts the claims of these false "faith healers." Where are those dead who were raised, and those desperate people who were cured of

---

71 William Nolen, *Healing: A Doctor in Search of a Miracle* as quoted by John McArthur, *Charismatic Chaos,* (Grand Rapids, Zondervan 1992) pp206-207. The bold face is ours for emphasis.

some terminal illness? Despite all the glowing press releases and other hype, they are nowhere to be found. Consequently, we are looking straight into the face of a monumental deception of the enemy. Even the unsaved can see through this fraud:

> James Randi, a professional magician, wrote a book in which he examines the faith healers. Randi is openly antagonistic to Christianity. Nevertheless, he seems to have done his investigation thoroughly and fairly. He asked scores of faith healers to supply him with "direct, examinable evidence" of true healings. "I would have been willing to accept just *one* case of a cure, so that I might say in this book that at least on one occasion a miracle occurred," he wrote. But not one faith healer anywhere gave him a single case of medically confirmed healing that could not be explained as natural convalescence, psychosomatic improvement, or outright fakery. Randi's conclusion? Reduced to its basics, faith healing today – as it has always been – is simply magic.[72]

James 5:15-16

Brrrrr, that's scary. Half the church is following after these so-called prophets. Scripturally, only the elders of the church are granted the authority to heal.[73] Seeking supernatural healing through an "anointed" human is not only unbiblical; it is downright dangerous. King Saul sought a prophetic message from Samuel, through a method condemned by the Lord. The outcome was disastrous. Carefully read 1 Samuel 28:7-20, paying special attention to vs.15-16. God has not changed. If the Lord does not will to heal us through the elders, seeking supernatural healing through another channel could also be disastrous! It would not be of God, and there is only one other source... a demon. Prophets in the Old Testament didn't have the indwelling Holy Spirit. Jesus changed that.

---

72 *ibid*, pp208-209. This account by an unbeliever is cited to show how exceeding the Scripture can give grounds for the world to ridicule the faith, and to question the reality of any Christian experience.

73 There is a colossal difference between a mother who implores the Lord to heal her sick child and someone who claims to have a special "anointing" which empowers him to heal the sick, or raise the dead. One is asking the Lord Himself to heal, the other is stating that he has been given supernatural power to heal. The first is biblical; the latter is not.

About Authority

These alleged "Christian healers," even using the name of Jesus, are presumptuously grasping for more glory, and more spiritual authority than the Bible grants. They are like the sons of Sceva, and are in the sin of Korah. King Uzziah exceeded his authority and recklessly went into the temple to offer incense and to worship God. He got leprosy for his efforts.[74] What God's judgment will be on these modem-day mediumistic spiritists, only He knows. But when it comes, it will surely be terrible and violent, just as the Black Plague was, on the eve of the reformation, when all Europe was in dark idolatry.

You see where all this is leading, don't you? Satan is training the churches to accept their final leaders on the basis of the supposed works they perform, rather than on what the Word of God tells us about the doctrines they teach. The enemy is educating the church to put feelings, personal experiences, and even counterfeit miracles, above the Bible. That is very important. Think on it awhile. Scripture tells us to test those who claim to be something special:

> Revelation 2:2 "I know your works... and that you cannot bear those who are evil. And you **have tested** those who say they are apostles and are not, and have found them liars;"

Do we do that? It doesn't seem so. In childlike simplicity, Jesus' little wandering sheep say, "Amen, Amen," to these false healer-prophets. The shepherds (their pastors) have not grounded them in the Word, and Satan leads them astray. In writing these things, I perceive that the Lord's hand will soon be very heavy upon the careless pastors, and my heart grieves for them. My soul longs for them to return to God, but they will not:

> Matthew 23:37 O Jerusalem, Jerusalem, the one who kills the prophets and stones those who are sent to her! How often I wanted to gather your children together, as a hen gathers her chicks under *her* wings, but you were not willing!

Woe to you shepherds, if you annul even the least of God's commands unto these little ones, and by so doing, you cause Jesus' precious sheep to stumble. I would rather be flayed alive, than be in your shoes when Jesus returns...as He will shortly:

---

74 Acts 19:13-15, Numbers 16:1-35, 2 Chronicles 26:16-21

Zechariah 11:16 **"For indeed...a shepherd in the land *who*... will eat the flesh of the fat and tear their hooves in pieces."**

(As hirelings, many pastors sell their services to the highest bidder. They feed themselves on Jesus' sheep, and do not teach the Bible. Without the pure water of the Word, the hoofs of Jesus' sheep are tom off, so they cannot walk the Christian walk.)

Zecharia 11:17 **"...A sword *shall* be against his arm...His arm shall completely wither,** (The sword of the Spirit, which is the Word of God, is no longer wielded with power; for the zeal for the Word of the Lord has withered, being displaced by the doctrines of men.) **"And his right eye shall be totally blinded."**

(Spiritual insight has been lost, and the eye of the heart has become dimmed. We have been separated from the truth by the black sackcloth of our iniquity.)[75]

And if you say that you didn't know that you were doing wrong... that you were just following orders... your denominational view: That is what the murderers of the martyrs said when they burned our brethren at the stake. That is what the Nazis said as they gassed and machine-gunned 6,000,000 Jews. You sound just like Goering, and Himmler, and Albert Eichmann, and all they did was kill the body. You are responsible to God for the immortal souls of the sheep He has placed in your care:

If you say,
"Surely we did not know this,"
Does not He who weighs
the hearts consider *it*?
He who keeps your soul,
does He *not* know *it*?
And will He *not* render to *each* man
according to his deeds?

Proverbs 24:12

75 The author is indebted to Randy N., a younger brother in the Lord, for an understanding of this puzzling passage in Zechariah. Usually considered to refer to a coming Antichrist, it appears that this passage is now being fulfilled right before our eyes. If we in the ministry are bound by our doctrinal traditions, we will be unable to hear the Holy Spirit as he speaks through the brethren.

CHAPTER TEN

Witchcraft

By now, the delusions we have talked about in previous chapters have taken the brethren so far from the Word that they are ready to swallow a really big lie, like: "If you don't speak in tongues, you're not saved." If your stated intent was to rob the glory from the cross of our Savior Jesus Christ, and give it to some false spirit, that doctrine would be the way to do it! Besides, it is Satan's old trick of "faith plus something." There is so much Scripture to refute that insanity, that the author is tempted to say, just go read your Bible. But additionally, let's take a little look at 19 centuries of church history. *Fox's Book Of Martyrs* records hundreds of accounts of the giants of the faith, who died for the Lord in tortures beyond imagining.[76] While being burned at the stake, saint after dear, suffering saint, with faces charred beyond

76 Two other works are must reading for every Christian who really wants to know what being a Christian is all about: *Martyrs Mirror,* (Scottdale, PA, Herald Press, 1950) and *The Pilgrim Church,* (Pickering & Inglis, Basingstoke, Hants, UK, 1931)

recognition, kept committing themselves "unto Him who is able," asking for the forgiveness of their sins, and the sins of their tormentors. Oh, those blessed, steadfast brethren. While their own smoking fat fueled the flames, they were holding burning arms toward heaven, praising God.

To suggest that these brethren were not filled with the Spirit is absurd... but not one of them is recorded as having "sought" for the Holy Spirit, or spoken in "tongues." Read the *Book of Martyrs* yourself. Most of those dear saints had complete victory over their pain. Is that not the gift, of miracles, or perhaps the gift, of faith? Listen to what happened to the much beloved preacher John Hooper of London, when he spoke out against the corrupt abuses of the mainline churches of his own day:

> On February 9th, 1555, at about eight o'clock, John Hooper was led forth, and many thousands of people were collected, being market day. He smilingly beheld the stake and preparation made for him.
>
> Command was given that the fire should be kindled. But because there were not more green fagots than two horses could carry, it kindled not speedily, and was a pretty while before it took the reeds upon the fagots. At length it burned about him, but the wind having full strength at the place, and it be a lowering cold morning, it blew the flames from him, so that he was in a manner little touched by the fire.
>
> A few dry fagots were brought, and a new fire kindled with fagots (for there were no more reeds), and those burned at his lower parts, but had small power above because of the wind, saving that it burnt his hair and scorched his skin a little. In the time of which fire, even as at the first flames, he prayed, saying mildly, and not very loud, but as one without pain, "O Jesus, Son of David, have mercy upon me, and receive my soul!" After the second fire was spent, he wiped both his eyes with his hands, and beholding the people he said with an indifferent loud voice, "For God's love, good people, let me have more fire." And all this while his lower parts did burn: but the fagots were so few, that the flames only singed his upper parts.
>
> The third fire was kindled which was more extreme than the other two. In this fire he prayed with a loud voice, "Lord Jesus, have mercy upon me! Lord Jesus receive my spirit!" And these were the last words he was heard to utter. But when he was black in the mouth, and his tongue so swollen that he could not speak, yet his lips went until they were shrunk to the gums: and he knocked his breast with his hands

> until one of his arms fell off, and then still knocked with the other, while the fat, water, and blood dropped out at his fingers ends, until by renewing the fire, his strength was gone, and his hand clave fast to the chain upon his breast. Then immediately bowing forward, he yielded up his spirit.[77]

Oh my God, how far we have fallen from the faith. We don't even know what it means to take the name of Christian. Can you imagine some arrogant, so-called "filled with the Spirit" zealot, with his hands in his pockets, presumptuously sauntering up to one of those precious burning brethren and sneering, "you aren't saved, you aren't speaking in tongues." Monstrous!

Yet today, there are evangelists with their hands in YOUR pockets, presumptuously sauntering up to a microphone and making similar heretical statements on nationwide television. The only difference is 400 years. There are still saints out there who are suffering for the Lord Jesus, and one would be hard-pressed to come up with a doctrine that would test their faith more:

> 2 Peter 2:1-3 ...there will be false teachers among you, who will secretly bring in destructive heresies... And many will follow their destructive ways, because of whom the way of the truth will be blasphemed. **By covetousness they will exploit you with deceptive words;**

These same television "prophets" are recklessly advising Christians to leave sound Bible-teaching churches if the "fullness" and "tongues" doctrines are not taught. They need a history lesson. No one told that to the estimated 4,000,000 saints who were killed by the Roman empire, or the countless millions martyred by the Roman church. Those true saints just put their trust in Jesus. Matter of fact, if we need a "tongue" (or some other spiritual marvel) to bolster our faith, then we haven't got faith at all.

> Hebrews 11:1 Now faith is the substance of things hoped for, **the evidence of things not seen.**

It isn't faith when we rely on some charismatic phenomenon we have seen, or on some "tongue" we have uttered. That's sight, and "...we

---

77 John Fox, Fox's Book of Martyrs (Grand Rapids, Zondervan, 1967) pp214-215.

walk by faith, not by sight." 2 Corinthians 5:7 *Faith is when one stands in a truth despite the odds,* just like the martyrs did:

Hebrews 11:6 **But without faith *it is* impossible to please *Him*...**

So again: Faith is when one stands on the truth despite the odds! The martyrs didn't "seek for the filling," or plead for some charismatic phenomenon to help them stand against the attacks of the enemy. They *knew* they were indwelt by the Holy Spirit because that's what the Bible told them. They went to the stake just trusting in Jesus; and brethren, what more is there to trust in than Him? If a saving faith in the Lord Jesus (which invariably leads to obedience to God's Word), and that faith *alone,* were sufficient to keep those brethren walking in the Lord, even at the cost of their lives, then an obedient faith *alone* is still good enough to keep the church standing against the terrible "persecutions" and "trials" we have today. Trials like staying out of topless bars, movies, TV., and too much frolicking on the beach. We are tragically spoiled spiritual babies, and God's discipline will be upon us shortly. Past, present, and future, "The just shall live by faith." just as Romans 1:17 says.

The issue here is not whether we can be filled with the Spirit subsequent to salvation, or even be given a greater gift. While teaching, I myself have been aware of the blessing and guidance of the Holy Spirit (because of its misuse, I don't use the term *full* or *filling* much anymore). What true Bible teacher hasn't? The real question is whether the Holy Spirit will continue to minister through us with signs and wonders when we disregard God's statutes, and openly display to the fallen angelic majesties that the church is not in submission to the Lord.

For instance: Will the Holy Spirit give a spiritual manifestation to a woman who does not have her head covered, is teaching or holding authority over a man, or is speaking out in church? If He were to do so, He would be going against His own inspired Word, which He also tells us is unchanging and everlasting.[78] If we conclude that the Holy Spirit will not go against His own Word, then where are these spiritual phenomena coming from? From whence cometh the charismatic sense of euphoria? A very good question. If it is not the Holy Spirit, there is only one other option: the enemy, a demon.

Some will ask, "Well, what about some poor woman who doesn't understand these submission commands, and doesn't realize that they

---

78 Isaiah 40:8, Psalm 119:60, 2 Timothy 3:16, 2 Peter 3:2, 15-16.

could be binding to her?" That was covered in footnote No.41. God will forgive an unintended misunderstanding of His Word, but this is something totally different. We are claiming that the Holy Spirit Himself is giving out these "tongues," and the Holy Spirit knows the Bible backward and forward. He inspired it! If He were to empower a woman to speak a tongue or prophecy in church, in opposition to what His inspired Word states, He would be speaking against Himself, and empowering someone to sin. That is impossible, James 1:13.

Incantations

Somehow, false doctrines feed on themselves. Churches rarely repent of their errors. Instead, new false rituals are added to support existing fables. In some congregations, there are all kinds of mediumistic procedures to help one "receive" the gift of "tongues"; anointings and special teachings on how to form tongue "words"; and special spirit worshiping seances called "fullness" conferences. You realize that all religious rituals not commanded by Scripture border on the practice of magic, don't you?[79]

The Holy Spirit is not a performing puppet, giving gifts on demand at some Sunday evening service. We forget that fire came forth from the Lord, and slew Nadab and Abihu for worshiping in a false spirit. We worship a holy and awesome God who is greatly to be feared. Moses, one of the most sanctified men who ever lived, was in great fear when he beheld Him.

> Acts 7:32 ...'I *am* the God of your fathers, the God of Abraham and the God of Isaac and the God of Jacob.' **And Moses trembled and dared not look.**

> Hebrews 12:21 And so terrifying was the sight, *that* Moses said, **"I am exceedingly afraid and trembling."**

Look out at those millions of stars, some of them thousands of light years away. Look at the awesome fury of a hurricane, or the boiling atomic cauldron of our own sun. The Lord God made them all. God Most High is the creator of the universe, who could snuff out this sinful planet with a thought. The Lord is not at our beck and call,

---

79 Deuteronomy 4:2, Deuteronomy 12:32, Proverbs 30:6, and Revelation 22:18 warns us not to add to God's commands. 1 Samuel 15:21-23 shows us how God views such excesses in worship.

casually handing out favors here and there, when we *(without even the fear or wisdom to spiritually cast our shoes from off our feet)* ring the Sunday evening "come get your tongues" bell. This awesome God, through His Spirit, gives gifts to *whom* He wills, *when* He wills. Our irreverent craving "for the filling" must be a stench in his nostrils.[80]

Come Holy Spirit

Sometimes in these meetings, special invocation songs are sung like, "Come Holy Spirit, I need you," followed by a period of silence, during which spiritual phenomena are sometimes observed in the congregation. Women have their hands raised and waving, and you hear people "praying in tongues" all over the place. Brethren, that is counter to the Scriptures, which state, "I want *men* in every place... to pray, lifting up holy hands... let women receive instruction with entire submissiveness," and, "tongues... should be by two, or at most three."[81]

On the surface, these services look so godly that the open heresy is not readily apparent. However, asking the Holy Spirit to come denies His presence! It denies the indwelling of the Holy Spirit in the individual believer! It denies that the Holy Spirit has already been given to the believer by God the Father! It denies that we are sealed by the Holy Spirit unto the day of redemption![82] Let me say that again:

> **Asking the Holy Spirit to come to us is an out-and-out denial that He is already indwelling the believer. This is calling God a liar, and totally disregarding a basic attribute of His divine nature. Calling up the Holy Spirit is an incantation, and that is *witchcraft!***

Saul fell into the same sin. He asked the witch of Endor to call up the spirit of Samuel. Saul wasn't calling up some evil spirit, but a prophet of the Lord. So it is not the kind of spirit we wish to contact,

---

80 Isaiah 65:5, 1Corinthians12:7, 12:11

81 1 Timothy 2:8,11, 1 Corinthians 14:27

82 Isaiah 57:15; John 7:38, 14:16-17, 15:26, 16:7; Acts 5:32, Romans 5:5, 8:1, 8:16; 1 Corinthians 3:16, 6:19; 2CO 1:22, 6:16; Galatians 3:2, 4:6; Ephesians 1:13,4:30; 1 Thessalonians 4:8; 2 Thessalonians 2:13; 2 Timothy 1:7; Titus 3:5; 1 John 2:20,3:24.

but *the incantation itself*, the calling up of any spirit, that is sin.[83] If we obey God's Word, the Holy Spirit will be *given* to us in full measure. We don't need to go looking for Him. He is the Spirit of God, and He is sent to us by the Lord Jesus, just as Scripture declares.[84]

In both the Old Testament and the New Testament, calling for Him is directly counter to how the Bible says we receive the Holy Spirit.[85] There are many more proof texts, but those cited in the footnote should be enough to satisfy all but the most hardened skeptic. Praise God, the Holy Spirit is always in the heart of the Christian. How do we know for sure? The Bible tells us so:

> John 14:16-17 "**And I will pray the Father, and He will give you another Helper, that He may abide with you forever – the Spirit of truth,** whom the world cannot receive, because it neither sees Him nor knows Him; but **you know Him, for He dwells with you and will be in you.**
>
> Hebrews 13:5 ...For He Himself has said, **"I will never leave you nor forsake you."**

Secret Languages

As if the foregoing errors were not sufficiently heretical, also claimed by many charismatics is a "prayer language." Paul refers to praying in tongues (in his spirit, 1 Corinthians 14:14-15) but this special "secret" prayer language, which all are taught to seek, is in theory some totally unintelligible heavenly tongue undecipherable to any hearer.[86] Supposedly, this "secret language" permits the individual's

---

83 Leviticus 19:31, 20:6, 27, Deuteronomy 18:11, 1 Samuel 28:8-25, Isaiah 8:19, 19:3.

84 John 14:16-24, 16:7-15, Acts 5:32

85 Nehemiah 9:20, Isaiah 44:3, John 14:16, 26, 16:7, Acts 5:32, Romans 14:17, 15:13-16, 1 Corinthians 2:12, Ephesians 2:18, 1:13

86 For a more detailed exposition of 1 Corinthians 14, see the exegetical note at the end of this chapter.

1 Cor 14:4
Read 1 Cor: 1-5 + verse 18, 27 & 28, 39

spirit to communicate with God.[87] There is neither biblical support, nor early church writings that suggest that believers would receive such a secret language; and from the following verse, the concept is openly unbiblical:

> 1 Corinthians 14:22 Therefore tongues are for a sign, not to those who believe but to unbelievers;

The purpose of the genuine gift of tongues is mandated by Scripture. It was given as a witness to the unsaved. It's pretty hard for tongues to be a sign to unbelievers, if they are uttered in some "heavenly language" that the unbeliever can't understand. In fact, just as Scripture says, an unsaved person would think you needed psychiatric help if you started witnessing to him in some "secret language," 1 Cor 14:23.

However, "secret languages" do have historic support, but guess where? In the ecstatic speech practiced by the mystery religions (particularly Mithraism) which were popular among the Roman soldiers of Jesus' time. Scripture shows those cultic practices to be demonic, 1 Corinthians 10:20.

But this is exactly the kind of clever scheme the enemy would like to get into the church. Why? Well, since "secret languages" are a secret, and a total mystery to all, who on earth can test them for authenticity?[88] The only New Testament tongues defined for us in the

---

87 Sometimes this "secret language" is received after the spirit seeker falls backward into a trance. This second phenomenon, called "slain in the spirit," is claimed to be the power of the Holy Spirit overwhelming the individual and rendering him unconscious. There is neither biblical nor apostolic support for this phenomenon.

88 This "secret language" fabrication is probably inferred from, "If I speak with the tongues of men or of angels," 1 Corinthians 13:1. The KJV translates the Greek *ean* (Strong's No.1437g) as "Though I were to speak...." But regardless of translation, *ean*, is a conditional particle. Paul did not state that he spoke in the tongues of angels, only what "if" he were to do so. Sort of like saying, "If I were to jump over the moon..." A hyperbole. This is a good example of a widespread spiritual deception based on a faulty interpretation of Scripture.

It might be thought that Paul prayed audibly in tongues from 1 Corinthians 14:14-15, but a careful analysis of context seems to indicate otherwise. See exegetical note on pp107-110.

Bible, were composed of known languages of men, understood by one or more of the hearers, Acts 2:6-11. In fact, the Greek word *glo_ssa* (Strong's No.1100g) which we translate "tongue," really means a language of man. Are "secret prayer languages" genuine spiritual phenomena? Some seem to be, but since they are not authorized by Scripture, whose spirit do you suppose is inspiring them?

Hot Line Doctrine

Further claimed by some, is that this "secret prayer language" is a direct *Hot Line* to God in heaven with which Satan cannot interfere. An unbelievable myth, with no scriptural support whatever. This again denies the indwelling Holy Spirit, or suggests that He is deaf, or that He has no communication with the rest of the Godhead, or that God does not know the thoughts and intents of our hearts, or that Jesus and God the..Father have not made their abode with us as John 14:23 states. More blasphemy![89]

The prayer language "Hot Line" doctrine again denies the omnipresence of God, which is directly against more Scripture.[90] Additionally, there are only two ways mentioned in the Word by which our prayers can be hindered, "If I regard iniquity in my heart," Psalm 66:18, or if a man mistreats his wife, 1 Peter 3:7.

Fullness Seance

It never seems to stop. New heresies continue to crop up. So-called "fullness" conferences are held, ostensibly for one to receive the fullness of the Holy Spirit. They didn't get that idea from the Word of God! There is no instance of such a conclave, for such a purpose, anywhere in the Bible. If we ought to have such a meeting, we would have a scriptural record of one, as an example. Furthermore, the Word states that the Holy Spirit was poured out when Jesus was glorified, Acts 2:33, and when we receive Jesus as our Savior, we are complete in Him, Colossians 2:9-10. Again, God the Father already has given us the Holy Spirit.[91]

---

89 Here are a few of the Scriptures: Psalm 94:11, 139:23, Isaiah 66:18, Matthew 9:4, Luke 11:17, Hebrews 4:2.

90 Job 38:4-33, Psalm 139:7-16

What then is the outcome of striving after the Spirit, counter to what Scripture directs, while also being in disobedience to the ordinances which show the fallen angels that the church is in submission to the Lord Jesus? The result is obvious. We have opened the church to direct satanic attack, and the judgment will fit the sin perfectly. We will get a "spirit" alright... lots of them!

91 I'm beginning to sound like a broken record, I know, but that is what the Bible says: John 14:16, Acts 5:32, 2 Corinthians 1:22, 1 Thessalonians 4:8.

Exegetical Note
1 Corinthians 14

To find truth, one must set prejudices aside, approach the Word of God with humility, and ask the Lord for the wisdom to discern His intent in a given Scripture. Affirmation from many brethren leads me to believe that the following is probably the correct exegesis of 1 Corinthians 14. However, this is a complex passage of Scripture, and some verses could be interpreted differently.

After Jesus was glorified, a new mode of worship was introduced. We know this new system as the New Testament church. 1 Corinthians chapters 11-14 contain the regulations for church assembly, 12:17, 14:26. The ordinances of head-covering and communion are explained in ch. 11. Spiritual gifts are described in chapters 12-13. The rules for assembly, and the proper use of the gifts are inaugurated in chapter 14. The Corinthian church was factious, 11:17, and it appears that the primary purpose of 1 Corinthians 14 was to bring unity to the Corinthian church, particularly in its exercise of the spiritual gifts.

Understanding ch.14 hangs on two questions: (1) What was Paul's intent in his use of the phrase "in the spirit"? (2) Why was *proseuchomai,* "praying" in tongues mentioned only twice,[92] while *laleo,* "speaking" in tongues was discussed 15 times.[93] All of 1 Corinthians 14:2-13 and 14:18-39 address speaking in tongues, while praying in tongues appears in only vs.14-15. Why?

> 1 Corinthians 14:5 I wish you all spoke with tongues, but even more that you prophesied; for he who prophesies *is* greater than he who speaks with tongues, unless indeed he interprets, that the church may receive edification.

It is apparent from v.5, that tongues and prophecies were both *spiritual revelations.* Prophecy was a revelation in a language understood by the assembly, while a tongue was a revelation in a language not understood by the assembly. Again from v.5, an interpreted tongue was equal in value to a prophecy; both edified the body. Despite charismatic doctrines to the contrary, from v.5 it seems that a tongue is

92 Greek, proseuchomai, defined to pray, Strong's No.4336g.

93 Greek: *laleo,* defined to talk, Strong's No.2980g.

a message from God's Spirit to man, and not a message from man's spirit to God!

> 1 Corinthians 14:13 Therefore let him who speaks in a tongue pray that he may interpret.

If v.5 is studied in conjunction with v.13, it appears that the tongue speaker was to pray for the interpretation of his own tongue, and *interpret his utterance himself.* This is strengthened by "...and let one interpret" of v.27 (i.e, his own tongue). The phrase is not, "and let *another* interpret." Note also the continued use of the singular personal pronoun "him" in v.28.

> 1 Corinthians 14:27-28 If anyone speaks in a tongue, *let there be* two or at the most three, *each* in tum, and let one interpret. But if there is no interpreter, let *him* keep silent in church, and let him speak to himself and to God.

That a person should interpret his own tongue is in keeping with a major theme of the Bible: A prophet was accountable for what he spoke "in the name of the Lord," Deuteronomy 18:20, Jeremiah 23:30, James 3:1, etc. We, too, are accountable before God for anything our mouth utters in His name (plain language or in a tongue). V.32 declares this accountability, "...the spirits of prophets are subject to prophets." The assumption that we can carelessly blurt out something we don't understand, from an unknown spirit, while claiming that it is from God the Holy Spirit, is not only unbiblical; it is presumptuous and spiritually dangerous:

> 1 Samuel 2:25 "If one man sins against another, God will judge him. But if a man sins against the LORD, who will intercede for him?"

Though Greek was the common language spoken during apostolic times, the Roman Empire was a highly mobile society, as evidenced by Acts 2:9-11, where speakers of at least 12 different languages were present. When we recognize that the saint should routinely interpret his own utterance, the separate gift of "the interpretation of tongues," 1 Corinthians 12:10, was probably the supernatural ability to translate for a foreigner who spoke in the assembly, rather than the ability of one Christian to divine the utterance of another member of the church who was speaking in some unknown "secret prayer language."

But the real key to 1 Corinthians 14 is in vs.14-15. Here we read about the spiritual activity taking place within two aspects of man's nature. A clear distinction is made between what is happening in: (1) the *pneuma,* or spirit,[94] and (2) the *nous,* or mind.[95] If a man prays in a tongue, he does so in his *pneuma,* "in the spirit" which can be understood to mean in his heart! If he receives no interpretation in his *nous* or mind, his mind is inactive, "my mind is unfruitful" v.14.

> 1 Corinthians 14:14-15 For if I pray in a tongue, my spirit prays, but my understanding is unfruitful. What is the *conclusion* then? I will pray with the spirit, and I will also pray with the understanding. I will sing with the spirit, and I will also sing with the understanding.

Nothing is said here about speaking aloud in tongues! We are reading about Paul's spirit and the mind, not his mouth. So how does a person pray and sing with the mind, v.15? Would that not be because he received the interpretation for his tongue in his mind? Simply stated, it seems that the tongue-speaker hears the tongue in his *pneuma,* or spirit, and receives the interpretation for it in his *nous,* or mind, v.15. When he both hears and understands his tongue, he prays and sings in both mind and spirit... and who wouldn't?

Paul, in his very precise use of *proseuchomai* (pray), and *laleo* (talk), appears to be making a distinction between what is happening in his heart, and what he is saying with his mouth. He did NOT speak his tongue out loud, unless he interpreted, v.16, because a person without his gift would not have understood what he was saying. It seems that the man granted an unknown tongue did not speak it aloud in the assembly; but instead, spoke a common language which could be understood by all. If a tongue-speaker did not understand his spiritual message, he was commanded to remain silent in the church, and "speak to himself and to God," v.28.

> 1 Corinthians 14:16-17 Otherwise, if you bless with the spirit, how will he who occupies the place of the uninformed say "Amen" at your giving of thanks, since he does not understand what you say? For you indeed give thanks well, but the other is not edified.

---

94 Greek: *pneuma,* defined as spirit, Strong's No.4151g.

95 Greek: *nous,* defined as mind, reason, or understanding, Strong's No.3563g

Pentecostals interpret the "my spirit prays" of 1 Corinthians 14:14-15, as license to pray *audibly* in tongues in the church. From this notion, many go on to teach that anytime praying or speaking "in the Holy Spirit" is mentioned elsewhere in the Bible, it also refers to praying audibly in tongues. A dubious concept at best, because vs.16-19 discourage such a practice. It seems that Pentecostals do not recognize that within the context of 1 Corinthians 14, *proseuchomai* (praying) refers to something taking place in the heart, while *laleo* (talk) refers to what is being spoken out loud! How did Jesus pray?

The concept of silent prayer is affirmed elsewhere in Scripture. In Ephesians, Paul defines praying "in the spirit" as silent: "*Speaking to yourselves in psalms and hymns and spiritual songs, singing and making melody in your heart to the Lord,*" Ephesians 5:19. The phrase "in your heart," is just another way of saying "in the spirit;" and there is no way that the "in your heart" of Ephesians 5:19 can be construed to mean audible prayer. Furthermore, "in the spirit" appears 16 more times from the epistles to Revelation, and all refer to an activity taking place within the heart.

So where is the scriptural support to interpret the "my spirit prays" of 1 Corinthians 14:14-15 as audible prayer? Nowhere! Try as he might, the author could not find a single verse that even hinted at *audible prayer* in an unknown tongue (or in a so-called "secret prayer language"), in the church, or anywhere else for that matter.

How saints should act when they assemble is the central theme of 1 Corinthians chapters 11-14. These four chapters contain the only place in the New Testament where the order of worship is set forth, 14:26-33. It is within this setting that the overall intent of chapter 14 becomes evident. 1 Corinthians 14 regulates what should take place silently, in an individual's heart, and what should be voiced audibly to the whole church. The Lord, through Paul, commanded the church to show some maturity in its exercise of audible tongues, v.20, and stated that tongues were not given for the believer's edification (though some took place 14:4), but as a sign to unbelievers, v.22.

So why has Satan gone to such an effort to get this false "praying in tongues" doctrine into the church? Because the enemy knows the true value of prayer. Praying is one of the strongest weapons the Lord has given us in our fight against the forces of darkness. If the saints can be deceived into believing that hours of meaningless babbling is prayer, then the church's effectiveness before the throne of grace can be destroyed.

What did Jesus show us in prayer?
He told the demons audibly to leave.
He gave us the Lord's prayer as an example.
He prayed out loud so the disciples would know how to pray. Jesus is our example.

CHAPTER ELEVEN

Mediums and Psychics

I am distressed by the accounts recorded here. Some of these brothers and sisters are personal friends. Their churches and pastors are well-known to me, and I love them all in the Lord. Some will never speak to me again.[96] Folks don't take kindly to the suggestion that they are being influenced by an evil spirit, but in each of the cited cases, that conclusion is· inescapable. If we continue to disobey openly the precepts that protect us from demonic influence, particularly after we have had them brought to our attention, then we are false prophets.

---

96 Written in 1985, this paragraph has come true, sad to say.

We have become wolves in sheep's clothing, teachers of futility, from whom God's people can derive no benefit, Acts 20: 29-30.

The Lord will not be glorified by citing a litany of all the errors coming out of the "seeking" for the Spirit movement. But examples of the three most apparent deceptions are discussed in full: (1) a false tongue and interpretation, (2) a false teacher, and (3) a false prophet.

A Tongue

There is historic support that genuine tongues have been spoken in the languages of man during the Christian Era. But God is not in the business of keeping the Gospel secret, revealing it only to an "anointed" few. The Lord wants all to hear the news about His dear Son. That is exactly what tongues were all about:

> 1 Corinthians 14:22 Therefore tongues are for a sign, not to those who believe but to unbelievers...

In the late 1600s, in the Cevennes mountains of France, there were simple believers so hated by the Roman church that the Pope ordered their extermination, calling them "the utterly detestable race of the ancient Albigenses." Some within this group were quite militant, defending themselves against the butchers sent against them by the Roman church; and they were much maligned, even by other Christians. Nevertheless, they may have had the scriptural gift of tongues:

> "Men and women fell into ecstasies, during which they spoke in the pure French of the Bible, whereas otherwise they could only speak in their own dialect, and they inspired their hearers with heroic courage."[97]

This is not a unique occurrence. The author has the tape of a message given by an old-time Mennonite revivalist. On it he tells of a series of tent meetings he held in Canada, and of a woman in one meeting who spoke nothing but French. Nevertheless, when he gave an invitation (in English) she was gloriously saved. On her way home her friends asked her how she understood what was said. To which she replied, "Ah, but he was speaking the most beautiful French." This dear old brother stated that this had happened twice in his ministry.

---

97 E. H. Broadbent, *The Pilgrim Church*, (Basingstoke, Hants, UK, Pickering & Inglis, 1931) pp232-233.

Then we have a letter from a pastor in Missouri who knew no Hebrew. But when witnessing to a Jewish boy, he said in Hebrew, "Joel, I am Jesus your peace." Three days later the boy was saved.

Mel Hendrix is a traveling missionary with a worldwide outreach. While riding in a taxi in Mexico, he was led of the Lord to witness to the cab driver. He started witnessing in English, but suddenly he was speaking in the driver's native language. Later, that taxi driver came to the Lord. So again:

> 1 Corinthians 14:22 ...tongues are for a sign, not to those who believe but to unbelievers...

Unfortunately, the account of the peasants of the Cevennes Mountains is rather sketchy. It was written in a time of severe persecution. But since it was recorded that they spoke in the "pure French of the Bible," it is reasonable to conclude that they were quoting the Bible. So the tongues of the Cevennes peasants, the Mennonite evangelist, the Missouri pastor, and Mel Hendrix all had three things in common:

1. All spoke a known language of man, understandable to the hearers.
2. All brought glory to the Lord Jesus.
3. All were signs to unbelievers.

But the vast majority of "tongues" spoken in churches today doesn't even sound like the same animal. These "tongues" are uttered in some unintelligible "secret language," spoken by women in disobedience to "let a woman cover her head... keep silent... not teach or hold authority over a man." And yet, some of these secret "tongues" appear to be supernatural phenomena. How can this be? Well, knowing that the Lord would not tempt anyone to sin, James 1:13, we have to ask, whose spirits would influence a woman to disobey God's Word? Here is what Randy Negaly. shared with me several years ago, and is also recorded in *Sunset:*

> In a local church a woman spoke in a "tongue." It was interpreted by the church's pastor as, "I was with you in darkness..." Brother, that interpretation was not "I was with you *while you* were in darkness," but "*I was with you* in darkness..."

So that "tongue" declared that the spiritual being who gave it was in darkness himself! Subtle, but then who is the prince of darkness? Certainly not the Lord Jesus, He is the light of the world. With the Lord there is no darkness at all. Just the entry of God's Word brings light. So whose spirit was with this woman while darkness remained around them both? Obviously a demon. As a result, rather than a gift of the spirit, we see that this woman was behaving as a medium. Her "tongue," therefore, was demonic! Interestingly enough, this identical tongue has been heard in several other churches, so this must be some common falsehood the enemy is using to confuse the saints. Jesus is not in darkness, brethren, because that is what the Bible says.[98]

Evil spirits control church services in several different ways, sometimes by influencing visiting celebrities. The following was told to me by Allen, a young brother who attends a Pentecostal church which prides itself on having a pastor who clings exactly to the Word:

> I attend a 3000 member Assembly of God. Last Sunday, a traveling pastor (I believe his name was Thompson) visited our church. He stood up to preach and said, "The Holy Spirit does not want me to preach out of this book today (holding up the Bible). Now all you tongue speakers start praying in tongues." And so it went for two more hours, as he kept pumping up the congregation. We just sat there while the tongue-speaking portion of the congregation stood waving their hands and speaking in tongues.
>
> Isn't that against the Bible, 1 Corinthians 14:26-27? There was no message, and no Bible reading. After the service was over, the visiting pastor said, "Now don't you feel good, you've just been involved in spiritual warfare." I didn't feel good at all. I was sick of the whole thing, but I go there because my wife speaks in tongues.

It was spiritual warfare alright, and that church lost. There was no Bible reading, no instruction, and the name of Jesus was not lifted up. And besides that, "Pastor" Thompson encouraged the church to sin. Just as Allen thought, that whole meeting was in disobedience to the written Word of God:

> 1 Corinthians 14:27-28 If anyone speaks in a tongue, *let there* ***be*** **two or at the most three,** *each* in turn, and let one interpret. But **if there is**

98 Ephesians 6:12, John 1:1-9, Ephesians 5:14, Psalm 18:28, Micah 7:8, Psalm 119:130.

Tongues need not be interpreted when praying but when a 'Word is given for the church

no interpreter, let him keep silent in church, and let him speak to himself and to God.

What is the matter with the church, that we go directly against the Word of God without fear and trembling. Were those tongues interpreted? If not, were those speakers silent in the church? If not, would God's absolutely righteous Holy Spirit be involved in their disobedience? The answer is obvious. This is very serious, and no game. There is no such thing as a "little" false tongue. A spiritual phenomenon is either of God the Holy Spirit, or it's of the devil.

Spirits Unmasked

Now for the bottom line. Saints with a ministry in deliverance will uniformly attest to one truth. Interact with satanic spirits long enough, and you will end up with one in residence! You say it couldn't happen to you? It happened to Sally, whose story you read in Chapter 3. Then a Baptist pastor's wife was seriously demonized after she "sought the filling," and spoke in "tongues".[99] And here is what just happened in Naples, FL. Mari Beth (a head-covering sister) of that city was counseling a young Baptist lady named Rachel who was in spiritual turmoil. Here is Mari Beth's story:

> Rachel loves the Lord, reads her Bible, and could speak in tongues at will. I asked Rachel if she had ever had her "tongue" spirit tested as commanded by 1 John 4:1-3: "Beloved, do not believe every spirit, but test the spirits to see whether they are from God... every spirit that confesses that Jesus Christ has come in the flesh is from God; and every spirit that does not confess Jesus is not from God..."
>
> Rachel conceded that she had not had her spirit tested in that way, and that she would like to have it done. We met a couple of days later in a prayer room at the church. After a short time of prayer, I asked Rachel to start speaking in tongues.
>
> While Rachel was doing so, I said in a quiet voice, "Spirit, in the name of the Lord Jesus, declare that Jesus Christ has come in the flesh." This spirit did not respond directly, but Rachel started speaking louder in tongues. Again I said, "Spirit, in the name of the Lord Jesus, declare that Jesus Christ has come in the flesh." Again, this spirit did not acknowledge Jesus.

---

99 Merrill Unger, *What Demons Can Do To Saints;* (Chicago, Moody Press 1977), pp. 81-84.

Now does it not strike you as strange, that a spirit (supposedly of God) would not confess Jesus? It did me. So I said, "Don't you see, Rachel, that this spirit cannot be of the Lord? It refuses to confess Jesus."

To which Rachel replied, "But in my mind this spirit is saying, 'I am lord.'"

I was almost deceived by that declaration, but just the night before an elder warned me that these demons are cunning, and could say something like that. So I pressed that spirit with, "Spirit, are you the Lord who died on the Cross, was buried, rose on the third day, and now sits at the right hand of Authority on high?"

The spirit within Rachel shrieked out, "Nooooo!" Rachel's face contorted, and hissing and snarling, she fell off her chair. Her hands twisted into unnatural claw-like shapes. She curled into a fetal position and whimpered, "Please help me get rid of this thing." I phoned Ray and Jill Darby and asked them to come assist me, and within an hour or so Rachel was completely free of that demon.

That is not an isolated case. It is just the latest incident that has been reported to the author. In one of his marvelous books about freedom from demonic influence, Dr. Neil T. Anderson records an almost identical case of demonic deception through the counterfeit gift of "tongues." In fact, it was by hearing of this account in *The Bondage Breaker*, that Mari Beth knew how to deal with the evil spirit within Rachel. Neil Anderson writes:

After a lengthy discussion about false prophets and teachers, Alvin admitted, "I think my problems began when I failed to test the 'gifts' of tongues and prophecy conferred on me by false teachers. Not only was I deceived, but I have deceived others myself."

"Would you be willing to put your gift of tongues to the test?" I asked. I assured Alvin that I was interested in putting the spirit to the test, not him. Alvin really wanted to be free of deception and right with God.

"Yes," he answered.

I instructed Alvin to begin praying aloud in his "spiritual language." As he began to chant an unintelligible prayer, I said, "In the name of Christ, and in obedience to God's Word, I command you, spirit, to identify yourself."

Alvin stopped in the middle of his chanting and said, "I am he."

At this point a novice may have been tempted to take off his shoes, thinking he was on holy ground. But I continued the test: "Are you the 'he' who was crucified under Pontius Pilate, buried, raised on the third day, and who now sits at the right hand of the Father?"

Alvin almost shouted the response: "No! Not he!" I led Alvin through a prayer renouncing Satan's activity in his life, and he was free from that deception.[100]

Pentecostal churches are not noted for making their errors or spiritual problems public; so one wonders, how many poor men and women in those congregations are now in bondage to some evil spirit through fake tongues? Since none of those churches observes the submission ordinance and associated commands, who among them can discern that what is happening to them is demonic, or have any idea of how to stop it. As an aside, Ray Darby later reported:

> Over the past four years, my wife and I have been involved in the deliverance of a few demonized saints. Sometimes it used to take days to do what the Lord now permits to be accomplished in just hours. We have now been present at three deliverances where there were women in the room with their heads covered, and the difference is dramatic.
>
> The demons immediately recognize that the saints are in submission to the Lord, and that the church has authority over them through Jesus Christ our Lord. We don't have to take all that time establishing our position in Christ, taking authority, and so on. By the covering, the evil spirits know that they have been defeated. I now recommend head covering for all Christian sisters.

The effectiveness of head-covering (when dealing with evil spirits) had been affirmed earlier through some brethren in the Midwest. In 1986, just after *Sunset of the Western Church* was released, the author received three separate phone calls from three different pastors in three different states. All said that demons were easier to expel and hated it when there was a woman in the room with her head covered. If the demons hate it so, then head-covering has to be far more important than most churches believe it to be.

Some of you dear sisters have not yet spoken in "tongues," and are wondering what sin you are in, or what "i" you haven't dotted, or "t" you haven't crossed. The Lord knows your heart, and that what you were seeking, you were seeking in good faith. He has been protecting you. Get down on your knees and thank God for His covering hand.

---

100 Dr. Neil T. Anderson, *The Bondage Breaker*, (Eugene, OR, Harvest House, 1990) pp159-160.

Dear Sister, before you turn your mind and body over to some unknown spirit, note first, that to the author's knowledge, not one church in obedience to the submission ordinance and associated commands has "tongues." That's right. I know of no church where the women cover their heads and remain silent, that has "tongue" speakers within it... *Not One!* What does that tell you? It would appear that as generally practiced in churches today, "tongues" is a false gift, given by lying spirits! The true sign of being filled with the Holy Spirit of God has always been (not tongues) but a heart desire to obey God's holy Word.[101] If we cannot hear the Holy Spirit through all the Scriptures in the footnote below, we need to examine the genuineness of our relationship to the Lord!

Testing the Spirits

There is an additional little delusion we should mention here. According to "spirit-filled" doctrine, testing or questioning these spirits (in any way) is considered to be blasphemy against the Holy Spirit. That is an outright lie of the devil. It is a lie! It is a lie! It is a lie! It is another deception that Satan would love to get into the church. It would keep him from being unmasked. We are COMMANDED to test the spirits. So again:

Test the spirits! 1 John 4:1

The truth is that the Holy Spirit of God has no problem at all confessing Jesus. That's what God the Father sent His Spirit here to do. One of the Holy Spirit's main reasons for being on Earth is to lead us to the Lord Jesus, John 15:26. Do charismatics test these spirits? Not that I've heard. Instead, the method used by most to determine whether or not a spirit is from God, is how they "feel" about it. They use what they believe to be a spirit of discernment. But, we are not told to use a spirit of discernment. That is not the test given to us in the Bible. Knowing that our feelings are deceptive, the Lord mandated the acid *verbal* test mentioned above:

1 John 4:1-3 "Beloved, do not believe every spirit, but test the spirits, whether they are of God; because many false prophets have gone out into the world. By this you know the Spirit of God: Every spirit that

---

101 John 16:13; Romans 8:13; Ephesians 5:9 (KJV); 2 Timothy 1:14; Hebrews 3:7-13; 1 Peter 1:2, 22.

> confesses that Jesus Christ has come in the flesh is of God, and **every spirit that does not confess that Jesus Christ has come in the flesh is not of God. And this is the *spirit* of the Antichrist,** which you have heard was coming, and is now already in the world."

I know these verses have been belabored to death, but it is imperative that the brethren get the message. Those who trust in subjective feelings for discernment, rather than the Word of God, are like sheep being led to the slaughter.

One tongue speaker believes that he has scripturally tested his own tongue. His spirit did not reply in English, but supposedly confessed Jesus in more tongues, followed by a good feeling. How could that be an adequate test? Any response from a spirit in more "tongues" (which you don't understand) is probably just further deception. The same thing went on in Rachel's mind. To test a tongue properly, the .person being tested must be speaking "in the spirit," at which time the person administering the test can address that spirit directly. But watch out, they will try to fool you. In Rachel's case, the evil spirit said to her mind, in English, "I am lord."

Identifying a so-called spirit of discernment (or prophecy) is tougher. Even though the prophet would be speaking in English, that person could be speaking "the imaginings of his own mind," or unknowingly be acting as a medium.

> Jeremiah 14:14 The prophets prophesy lies in My name. I have not sent them, commanded them, nor spoken to them; they prophesy to you a false vision, divination, a worthless thing, and the deceit of their heart.

One has to wait until the spirit of discernment is being evidenced, and then verbally command that spirit to conform to 1 John 4:1-3. These are cunning and deceptive spirits, with thousands of years of experience in fooling man. Unmasking them is not all that easy, but when a spirit is tested properly, dramatic things sometimes happen. During the seven years since *Sunset* was written, I know of only a half dozen spiritual manifestations that appear to have passed the above scriptural test. I know of hundreds that have not. Consequently, we should accept NO spiritual phenomenon as being of God, unless the spirit behind it conforms to 1 John 4:1-3. We do have a wonder-working God, who can decree a spiritual gift at any time He wills, but He will not enact a single miracle outside the precepts of His written Word.

Some declare that God can operate outside the guidelines of Scripture. They claim that those who think otherwise "are putting God in a box." What an absurd concept, as if the attitudes or ambitions of mortal man could keep the Creator of the universe from doing anything He wills. The Bible tells us who the Lord is, and what His will is. It tells us of His thoughts, His plans, His holiness, His very nature. God cannot depart from His Word, because if He were to do so He would be departing from His nature. To bring it all into focus: Would a true Christian live in adultery? Of course not, it would go against the new heart the Lord has given to the saints, Ezekiel 36:26. It would go against the Christian's new nature. In the same way, the Lord cannot do something that would go against His written Word *(no matter how minor)* because He would have to go against His own holy and unchanging nature to do so, Hebrews 13:8.

Attacks in the Flesh

Some time ago I corresponded with Fritz Z. (a brother in Holland) about his charismatic experience, and the physical troubles that followed. He received his "tongues" through some European charismatic group. During the course of our correspondence, he wrote some of the most blasphemous letters it is possible to imagine; and yet he claimed to be "filled with the spirit," as evidenced by speaking in "tongues." He wrote in one of his more gentle letters:

> "Several months ago I was trying to help a Christian sister get rid of a demon that she obviously had. As I was praying, this demon attacked my jaw muscles so severely that it hurt me to speak. My jaw has been giving me trouble ever since."

By his own declaration, an evil spirit attacked Fritz's jaw while he was trying to free a woman from another demon. This attack to the jaw is particularly significant; because Sally of Chapter 3, was also attacked in the jaw. Both of these believers spoke in "tongues," and both were physically attacked in part of the speech mechanism while so doing. That is probably more than just coincidence. If their "tongues" were satanic, their speech mechanism would have been under direct demonic control. In both of these cases, that demonic control appears to have become a lasting affliction... an attack on the central nervous system, as Neil T. Anderson documents in *The Bondage*

Breaker.[102] The tragedy is that they both may still have the evil spirits that caused their distress. In Sally's case I was too inexperienced to help; but with Fritz I really tried, carefully walking him through the Scriptures. He was too deceived to hear them.

Some time later, I went back to see Sally, that demonized Pentecostal lady of Chapter 3, and directed her to wear a covering when praying or prophesying, that it would be a protection to her. She grasped that little straw of counsel like a drowning person, and I pray that the Lord used it to lead her to freedom. It was not all I should have done; but at the time, it was all I knew to do. Now I know that a demon is probably still with her unless she has totally renounced the sin of her involvement with the occult.

I haven't been back to that Assembly of God for several years now. From what I hear, they are still not submitted to the Word, and women are still speaking in "tongues," with heads uncovered. By now, some well-meaning soul has probably convinced that unfortunate lady that head-covering was only for the 1st Century Corinthians. I wonder how she is, and how many more there are like her in those churches.

More charismatic believers are now telling of undiagnosed physical problems afflicting them. One Christian Jewish woman, whom I know personally, claims to be a prophetess. She also adamantly refuses to cover her head. Since Scripture specifically commands a woman to cover her head when prophesying, 1 Corinthians 11:5-6, if this woman were to get a message from the spirit world, it could not be coming from the Holy Spirit of God. The point being: this poor lady now has a serious illness; and though she has been to many doctors, her condition remains undiagnosed. Her ailment and her prophecy could be coming from the same place: A demon.

If these open attacks on the flesh of professing Christians who are charismatic mean what they seem to mean, then it appears that the mere act of exhibiting a spiritual phenomenon that is not of God gives grounds for a demonic attack on the flesh! I wish I knew what to do for these troubled people; but if they resist what the Lord Himself has written in His holy Word, what can anyone do? If they cannot hear Moses and the prophets, they cannot hear the words of this book.

So if a woman who has her head covered gets a serious illness like cancer where does that come from and what is she supposed to do to get rid of it? It's from the

102 Neil T. Anderson, *The Bondage Breaker*, (Eugene, OR, Harvest House, 1990) pp111-112.

fallen world that we live in. No one will be exempt.

James 1:6
Believe in John 14:12-14 we don't tak[e] power over the Holy Spirit but we as[k]
We have not because we ask not.

A Teaching

There was a woman going into local churches with head uncovered, who stood before mixed congregations and "taught" the gift of healing. First: A gift of the Holy Spirit is *His gift!* He sovereignly decides *when* and *who* gets *what,* 1 Corinthians 12:7-11. To state that healing can be taught, is to imply that we have some sort of power over the Holy Spirit, to give us on demand, the gift we want. The grossness of that presumptuous blasphemy defies imagination. Second: The Holy Spirit still, again, and forever will not guide anyone to disobey the Word. The Bible says "Let a woman cover her head... keep silent... not teach or hold authority over a man."

Since that is what the Word states, and the Lord will not empower anyone to disobey it, James 1:13; if any supernatural healings were to take place through this woman, it would not be the Holy Spirit of God who was doing them. The only other source would be demonic, through a professed Christian behaving as a medium! This, while being deluded into believing she had a ministry for the Lord Jesus. The author believes there are many women who have been so deceived, among whom are such notable Pentecostals as Marilyn Hickey and Kathryn Kuhlman. One could reasonably ask, "Why would Satan lead someone to do counterfeit cures in Jesus' name?"

First: When the supposedly healed person finds that he is still ill, his faith in the Lord is shaken. That is so important it needs to be expanded on. When some misshapen paralytic brings his wheelchair up to one of these "healers" thinking that he is before a genuine servant of God, and nothing happens; he doesn't blame the phony faith healer, he blames God. Guess what, so does the faith "healer." The "healer" says, "It's not my fault you didn't get well, it's the Holy Spirit's." Or the "healer" says, "You didn't have enough faith." Thus blaming his own presumption on God, or on the ailing person who came to him for help. What terrible heartache these so-called "healers" have to answer for.

Second: There's the Trojan horse principle. That hollow wooden horse was brought into an impregnable walled city because the Trojans thought it was of the gods. Instead, it was full of soldiers who opened the gates of Troy to its enemies. What a striking resemblance that is to what is happening in the church today. A whole generation of women now point with awe to Marilyn Hickey and Kathryn Kuhlman as their authorization to disobey 1 Corinthians 11:5-10, 14:34-35 and

1 Timothy 2:11-12, thus putting the unverifiable works of a couple of disobedient women above the voice of God! And so, Revelation 2:20-24 is fulfilled right before our eyes, as we "...tolerate the woman Jezebel, who calls herself a prophetess, and... teaches and leads My bond-servants astray..." As we too learn "the deep things of Satan."[103]

A Word of Knowledge

At a local "fullness" conference, a pastor stood and gave a "word of knowledge," that another pastor who was there should go kneel at the altar. Supposedly, the women of the church were then to come forward, lay hands on him, and pray over him. Some young and humble pastor did so; but on the face of it, that "word" was counter-scriptural, 1 Timothy 2:12. Understanding that man is a type of Christ, and women are a type of the church, the implication of that "word" is clear: that the church has authority over, and needed to pray for Jesus. That's blasphemous! Just the opposite is true:

> Hebrews 7:25 Therefore He is also able to save to the uttermost those who come to God through Him, **since He always lives to make intercession tor them.**

Jesus continually prays for the church. If we needed to pray for Jesus, we would be without any hope at all. Was that "word" of the Holy Spirit? The answer is tragically obvious. It was demonic. That man was not speaking a word from the Lord. Instead he was behaving as a spiritist, a psychic. He was in touch with the occult. Do you realize how sick it makes me to write of these things? Praise God, Jesus won the battle on the cross! His blood needed to be sprinkled on the mercy seat for us all, just once. Jesus now sits at the right hand of the Father, and His name is "far above... every name that is named, not only in this age but also in that which to come," Ephesians 1:19-23.

There are dubious "words of knowledge," like the above, and there are words of KNOWLEDGE! As we have said before, there is an immeasurable gulf which separates the genuine from the counterfeit.

---

103 Dr. William Nolen in *Healing, A Doctor's Search for a Miracle,* was unable to report even one verifiable miraculous cure, from any organic disease, which could be credited to the Kuhlman crusades. John McArthur, in *Charismatic Chaos,* writes that he was unable to find even a single documented miracle performed by anyone within the charismatic, Pentecostal, or Third Wave movements.

It's pretty easy to tell the difference. Listen to the words of a nameless martyr in Italy in 1560:

> A young Englishman, who happened to be in Rome, was one day passing by a church, when the procession of the host was just coming out.[104] A bishop carried the host, which the young man perceiving, he snatched it away from him, threw it upon the ground, and trampled it under his feet, crying out: "Ye wretched idolaters, who neglect the true God, and adore a morsel of bread!"[105]

If ever during the Christian Era we are to hear the words of the Holy Spirit spoken through the mouth of mortal man, that would be the time. That young man gave his life for only 14 words. He knew they would kill him for it. He was a merchant traveling in Italy during a time when killing Protestants was a way of life there. Yet the Holy Spirit empowered him to be a mighty witness for the truth. Not a prophet of the Old Testament was more bold than he. The pope ordered him to be suitably tortured and then burned at the stake.

> When he heard the sentence pronounced, he implored God to give him the strength and fortitude to go through it. As he passed through the streets, he was greatly derided by the people, to which he said some severe things regarding the Romanish superstition. But a cardinal, who attended the procession, overheard him, and ordered him to be gagged.
>
> When he came to the church door where he trampled on the host, the hangman cut off his right hand, and fixed it on a pole. Then two tormentors, with flaming torches, scorched and bumed his flesh all the rest of the way. At the place of execution, he kissed the chains which were to bind him to the stake. A monk presented the figure of a saint to him, he struck it aside, and being then chained to the stake, fire was put to the fagots, and he was soon burned to ashes.[106]

---

104 According to the Roman Catholic doctrine of the "real presence," after the priest blesses the bread during the mass, it becomes the real flesh of Jesus. During the Middle Ages, this bread was then carried around the city and all the people would bow down before it and worship it.

105 John Fox, *Fox's Book of Martyrs,* (Grand Rapids, Zondervan, 1967) p104

106 *Ibid.*, pl05

Every time I get a little puffed up, and think I'm doing something for the Lord; I remember that young Englishman; and I also remember what the Lord said through the writer of Hebrews:

> Hebrews 11:36-38 Still others had trial of mockings and scourgings, yes, and of chains and imprisonment. They were stoned, they were sawn in two, they were tempted, were slain with the sword. They wandered about in sheepskins and goatskins, being destitute, afflicted, tormented – of whom the world was not worthy. They wandered in deserts and mountains, *in* dens and caves of the earth.

> Hebrews 12:4 You have not yet resisted to bloodshed, striving against sin.

To put this all in perspective, would any of today's "prophets," or "words of knowledge" speakers, be willing to shed his blood for his words? Would the "tongue" speaker be willing to die for his utterance? Would the man who told that pastor to go forward and have the women pray over him be willing to die for his saying? If those were God's servants, and those were really God's words, they would be; just as millions of martyrs were willing to die for what is written in the Bible.

Brother or sister, if you are not willing to die for what you are saying "in the name of the Lord," for the sake of your soul, don't say it. Speaking falsely in the name of the Lord is claiming that yours, or Satan's words, are the words of the Holy One of Israel. It is presumption. It is blasphemy against the God of Heaven:

> Ezekiel 13:3,6-8 Thus says the Lord GOD, "Woe to the foolish prophets, who follow their own spirit and have seen nothing! They have envisioned futility and false divination, saying, 'Thus says the LORD!' But the Lord has not sent them; yet they hope that the word may be confirmed. Have you not seen a futile vision, and have not spoken false divination? You say, 'The LORD says,' but I have not spoken." Therefore thus says the Lord GOD: "Because you have spoken nonsense and envisioned lies, therefore I *am* indeed against you," says the Lord GOD.

But despite the biblical warnings, people do it anyway. The church is being deceived by a stupendous magic show. Satan's goal today is to demonize the whole church. As we play with his spirits, we are playing into his hands. It will not be long before he demands payment for the little ditties he is fiddling for us, the tunes to which we are so rapturously dancing. The wonder is that we are not more demonized than we are. Thank God for His covering hand, His loving kindness and His mercy.

These few little accounts of false gifts are just the tip of the iceberg. As our land gets further from the Lord, demonic forces usually associated with Africa or the Far East, are now taking up their abode here. We have imported them, just like AIDS, Asian flu and the Indian guru. The sad truth about all this is that the Lord has given us impregnable defenses against demonic oppression, but we neither teach nor employ them anymore:

1. The head-covering ordinance of 1 Corinthians 11:3-15.
2. Women's silence of 1 Corinthians 14:34.
3. Women not to take authority over men of 1 Timothy 2:12.
4. The test for evil spirits, of 1 John 4:1-3.

That is partly what the Bible is for, to keep us from going off into error. For a spiritual experience to be of the Holy Spirit of God, it must line up with the Word of God.

So how do we help the brethren in deep spiritual trouble because of bogus spiritual gifts, when they are absolutely convinced that what they have is of the Lord? How do we combat the delusion? One can know and teach the truth, but how do we reach Sally and Fritz and hundreds like them in a way that they can hear? I wish I knew. Those being deceived by demonic spirits through false "tongues" are exceptionally difficult to reach. Even when Bible verses are quoted that are point blank against the most outlandish beliefs and practices, many will continue to believe what their familiar spirits tell them.[107] Worshiping God in a false spirit, just like Nadab and Abihu; demanding more spiritual authority, just like Korah. A sister in New England writes about her experience in the New Age, before she was saved:

> When I was in yoga, I attended a two day "intensive" during which one supposedly received an awakening of spiritual energy. This energy was said to be transferred by a thought, or a look from the guru, or "touch" to

107 Mark 3:24, 1 Corinthians 14:37-38, James 4:7, 2 John 9

your forehead by him.[108] People would then experience spiritual marvels such as roaring like lions, strange breathing patterns, or quirky movements.[109] One woman started speaking in tongues. The guru conversed with her a few times (from across the room) in what I believe was Hindi. This isn't just something I just heard about; I was there, saw it, and was myself involved. Despite all those wonders, no fruits of the Holy Spirit (Galatians 5:22-23) were in evidence. In fact, just the opposite was true; they were egocentric, rude, unkind, and unloving. Looking back, I am horrified at my participation in these mystic practices, and hate even to remember them. I now understand that all that I was involved in was demonic. I have renounced all my association with the works and forces of the enemy, and claim the blood of Jesus.

After I was saved, I went to a Pentecostal church for a little while. They also spoke in tongues. Having come to the Lord Jesus from the New Age where those things go on all the time, I knew it was wrong, but nobody would listen to me. The charismatics are doing the same things the unsaved are doing at yoga awakenings. Thank you, 0 Lord Jesus, for leading me out of that darkness into your marvelous light.

The enemy *(masquerading as the Holy Spirit)* is now having a field day in the church. However, Satan's arrogant delusion is instantly exposed when we obey the submission ordinance and associated commands, and test those spirits. God help us to see this spiritual battle clearly, and may the Spirit of the Lord Jesus protect us all. Demonic powers have now invaded the local churches, and many of them stand behind the pulpit. Sad to say, I found a few.

---

108 Charismatics call entering this state "being filled with the spirit." This condition is sometimes accompanied by a fainting phenomenon called "being slain in the spirit." Like the guru, charismatic leaders employ a "touch" to people's foreheads to cause this "Christian" experience. Some charismatic leaders pride themselves on their ability to cause whole sections of their audience to swoon by puffing in their direction. A similar fainting phenomenon was observed in early Frank. Sinatra concerts.

109 Charismatics sometimes exhibit this last phenomenon while dancing "in the spirit."

CHAPTER TWELVE

Deceiving Spirits

While driving around the countryside, I visited a charismatic church leader in his home. After our talk, we stood for prayer. The man asked me to lead, and then took hold of my hands and started to pray in "tongues". My mind was suddenly filled with all kinds of perverted, vile and lustful thoughts. I immediately placed myself under the blood of Jesus, and "brought every thought into captivity to Christ". Still, it was very hard to concentrate on my prayer to the Lord.

I didn't understand what was happening then, but I believe the Lord permitted me to understand what that tongue was saying, and where that spirit was from. I didn't *seek* for interpretation of tongues, it appears that God just *gave* it, when needed, for His child's protection and edification. Why then? Because there was no way (in the natural man) that anyone could have known that he was hearing from the enemy. The man himself sounded and looked just great, and one could believe that his charismatic display was a genuine gift of the Holy Spirit, the gift of tongues.

Be concerned for that man. He teaches the gospel (somewhat watered down) but he has gone astray. He might be horrified if he knew what the Lord had permitted me to see. But more likely, he wouldn't believe it. If he were made aware, would he give up his familiar spirit and repent? Probably not. Experience has shown that most Pentecostals will not give up their spirits, regardless of where those spirits are from, or what the Bible says.

The charismatic euphoria is a kind of deadly spiritual narcotic! But it feels so good that the addicting bondage cannot be perceived until too late.

Many charismatics know in their hearts the truth of that statement! Some have even told me that way down in their souls there was a little voice that kept warning them that they were doing wrong. The Holy Spirit graciously cautions the saints when they go off into error.[110] But Satan is very cunning. If one were to ask a charismatic who that "still small voice" of warning was, he would say that it was the devil trying to "steal your gift," and he'd tell you not to listen to it. It seems that the Pentecostals are attributing that quiet convicting voice of the Holy Spirit to the enemy! A frightening blasphemy.

Several years ago, I was sharing the Scripture on another subject with a different Pentecostal pastor. We disagreed, not about doctrine directly, but about whether certain verses in the Bible meant exactly what they said. I asked if we could go before the Lord on the matter. He refused, and suddenly asked, "How come my spirit doesn't witness to that?" It was a question that totally confused me until years later when the Holy Spirit turned on the lights. If someone's spirit does *not* witness to the written Word of God, that spirit is *not* the Holy Spirit of God. God's Spirit *will* always witness to His Word! Thus, the spirit by which that pastor was being influenced was a demon.

The Hierarchal System

Because churches do not purge themselves of pastors in open rebellion to the Bible, sin enters the assembly. But how did the church get so far from the truth? In many cases men who started out as

110 I attended an Assembly of God for a year and a half, and embraced their doctrinal position wholeheartedly. I spoke in "tongues" there for about six months. Thankfully, the Holy Spirit kept warning me that I was in error. My "tongues" were accompanied by a disquiet of spirit and a sense of oppression, and I lost the reality of my prayer life. Then I studied the Word and realized that this "gift" was "received" in a church which was in total disregard to the submission ordinance, and associated commands. I have long since renounced my departure from the faith, and have repudiated the sin of Nadab and Abihu in my life. Under the blood of Jesus, I pray that I give the enemy no more access. Now I say in the English tongue, "Jesus Christ has come in the flesh." 1 John 4:2.

servants of the Lord have allowed the enemy to lead them into being servants of *the system*. Satan wages one of his most subtle attacks in the environment of struggling to get ahead in the "church world." Such striving is certainly not biblical, and cannot escape demonic energjzation. This is how it works:

To get a bigger church, a young pastor needs his church to speak well of him, so he forgets that his first priority is to be true to God's Word in what he teaches. He is fearful of the denominational authorities who are eyeing his every move. He forgets that it is the Lord God Almighty (who owns the cattle on a thousand hills) whom he serves, and starts worrying about his earthly "pastorate." So he shades a little truth here, or bends his commitment to the Lord there. In a David Wilkerson survey, this attitude is affirmed by pastors themselves:

> Several very honest pastors wrote and said, "David, some of us do not dare to preach a hard reproving message because we fear for our future. When you have a family to support and you know the church board will not stand for much reproof, you soft-peddle it... Also it seems that you can grow faster by preaching a message that makes people feel good. It is the fear of the people and the need for security that hinders much holiness preaching today."[111]

By putting their salary from men above their service to God, the pastors condemn themselves, James 3:1. But if a pastor empties the church by teaching about sin, repentance, and the Christian walk, he'll never get ahead. So (except for a little handful of godly men) a pastor learns how to honey up his sermons. He attempts to make God acceptable to man, rather than warning the lost if they don't repent that they will spend an eternity in hell's fire. Each compromise he makes leads him further from the truth, and the higher he rises, the more compromises he makes to get there. His congregation loves him for it. They hear, "God is love, and we're all under grace. Just say the sinner's prayer, and we'll all go to heaven. No repentance from sin or godly walk required." That's a message most congregations will gladly receive, but it doesn't save anyone.

Finally, this much-loved and "successful" pastor gets a huge church with several associate pastors, or he goes to denominational headquarters. Now he has "power." It's only earthly power, to be sure, but from his exalted position he passes down his personal views as

111 David Wilkerson letter, *9-7-1992, (World Challenge,* Lindale, TX)

doctrines and edicts to which other young pastors have to submit. Now he keeps his eagle eye on them, and their jobs are on the line. If the new men do not conform to what this "church leader" thinks *his* church should be, then they're out of a job. It's the papal heresy all over again, but this time dressed in middle-class Protestant suits and ties:

> Malachi 2:7-9 "For the lips of a priest should keep knowledge, And *people* should seek the law from his mouth; For he is the messenger of the LORD of hosts. But you have departed from the way; You have caused many to stumble at the law; You have corrupted the covenant of Levi," says the LORD of hosts.

Most heresies don't come up from the people, they come down from the leadership; and church history shows that once false doctrines are in place, they are almost impossible to eradicate. Some denominational churches teach so much error (or are so demon-influenced) that their power to lead the lost to Jesus is gone. As each new leader rises in the system he adds his own wrinkles to the earthly doctrines with which his denomination is already saddled. Eventually, God rejects these leaders, too, from being kings over Israel. A new David is anointed, and a new body of believers springs up. But not this time. Now there are too few who care, and spiritual darkness descends upon the land:

> Luke 11:52 and Hosea 4:6 "Woe to you lawyers! For you have taken away the key of knowledge. You did not enter in yourselves, and those who were entering in you hindered." My people are destroyed for lack of knowledge.

Deceitful Spirits

All of this would be of little consequence if these were isolated incidents. But not understanding God's Word on these matters, and being busy with worldly concerns, most of the shepherds are not standing firm in the Scripture, and the sheep are confused. Hearing of all the "miracles" taking place in the church down the street, younger saints think they are missing out on some great blessing. So looking for the most spectacular spiritual fireworks, they go church-hopping. The devious hand of the enemy in all this commotion cannot be overlooked, as one traveling Bible teacher recounts:

A couple of years ago I was talking with Pastor Mac. He's an independent Baptist pastor in Florida, who was being influenced by the Pentecostals in his area. At the time, Pastor Mac was also involved in the deliverance of a demonized man. Mac told me that the demon within the man said that it would not come out, unless Mac drove it out by speaking in "tongues." Pastor Mac accepted what that demon said, and told me, "I guess I better learn to speak in tongues, huh."

I was really shaken! There can be only one answer to that. Pastor Mac knew it was a demon talking to him, and all demons are liars. Since when did we start getting our doctrines from demons? Where does it say in the Word that demons are subject to "tongues?" The Bible says that demons are subject to the Name of Jesus.

But I have to ask you this: Why would that demon have advised Pastor Mac to speak in tongues, unless by him doing it, he would be helping the kingdom of darkness? You know, obvious as it seemed to me, Pastor Mac was so fooled by the enemy that he couldn't see it. The enemy mixed up his mind, and led him into serious spiritual falsity.

I gave Pastor Mac a copy of *Sunset of the Western Church* and left. I said that it might answer some of his questions. Later, I came for another visit. I asked if he had read the book. "No," he said, "The spirit has not led me to." So now I have to ask you this one: Whose spirit would lead a pastor not to read a book which would influence him to obey the Bible? I knew, and went away feeling pretty bad. Mac has probably gotten his secret prayer language by now.

But that doesn't sound so disturbing, does it? The whole church seems to be headed that way. Maybe, but it's still a catastrophe. That man stands today in front of some of Jesus' little sheep who look to him for solace for their bruised and troubled hearts. But how can anyone who is leading people to a spirit be of help to those who need the healing power of Jesus?

Spirit of Antichrist

To date I have heard hundreds of "tongues," and dozens of words of knowledge and prophecies, supposedly spoken in the Holy Spirit. I cannot remember a single interpreted "tongue," word of knowledge, or prophecy, that declared that "Jesus Christ is come in the flesh." *Not one!* You would think out of 350 or so spiritual manifestations that at least *one* would have confessed His name.

That is of monumental importance! If a spirit does not confess Jesus as the Christ, right up front, he is not of God! Instead he is the spirit of Antichrist. How can we be so sure? Because that is what the Bible says:

> 1 John 4:2-3 By this you know the Spirit of God: **Every spirit that confesses that Jesus Christ has come in the flesh is of God, and every spirit that does not confess that Jesus Christ has come in the flesh is not of God.** And this is the *spirit* of the Antichrist, which you have heard was coming, and is now already in the world.

Consequently, who are these spirits speaking forth in "tongues" and "prophecies," who do not conform to this Scripture? They are demons! That's not all. Our bodies are the temples of the Holy Spirit. These familiar spirits are entering saints and declaring themselves to be God the Holy Spirit. How can we know? Read the following astonishing verse.

> 2 Thessalonians 2:4 ...who opposes and exalts himself above all that is called God or that is worshiped, **so that he sits as God in the temple of God, showing himself that he is God.**

Again, that is exactly what these familiar spirits are doing. They are entering professing Christians and claiming to be the Holy Spirit of God. May the Eternal God, the Father of Spirits, open our hearts to understand the real meaning of this passage in 2 Thessalonians 2. Antichrist is not whom we suppose. We don't need to go to some world capital, or the old temple site in Jerusalem to find him. The spirit of Antichrist is speaking in "tongues," right now, in our own churches. Are our spiritual ears open to hear this? It doesn't seen so. We would rather listen to our familiar spirits or stand on dead tradition. But we don't have to stay that way:

> Isaiah 59:1 Behold, the LORD'S hand is not shortened, That it cannot save; Nor his ear heavy, That it cannot hear.

If you are now experiencing some charismatic phenomenon, submit to the ordinances of God. Then ask some brother to command that spirit within you to declare that "Jesus Christ is come in the flesh" as you have read here. Be concerned enough about your own spiritual welfare to put your resident spirit to the test, exactly as God commands, 1 John 4:2-3. See if your "gift" continues.

Lead your family, your friends, your church into obedience to God's Word, and see if their spiritual phenomena continue. If your church is unwilling to submit to the ordinance of 1 Corinthians 11:5-6; and the statutes of 1 Corinthians 14:38, and 1 Timothy 2:8-15, do not be deluded as to whose spirit is influencing them to go against the Bible. If they continue in rebellion after understanding these truths, don't be fooled about which side is controlling their minds and hearts. And don't get puffed up, oh egotistical man, if your dear humble wife does cover her head. Get down on your knees and thank God with all your heart. Husbands are one flesh with their wives, Genesis 2:24, and when she submits to God's Word, she also shows her husband's submission, Ephesians 5:31. She protects her husband, too, from demonic influence.

Can we claim to be God's servants, and love Jesus, if we are unwilling to take so small a stand... just obedience to three little commands that cost us nothing. They are not going to burn you at the stake for it! Not yet, anyway. Think of Augustine the baker, Leonhard Keyser, John Hooper, and that young Englishman. Remember the martyrs who died to get God's Word to us in our own language. Then get down on your knees and explain to Jesus all your reasons for not wanting to obey it. Try out those 17 excuses on the Lord, and see how He likes them. Terrible things happen in our spirits if we hold the truth in unrighteousness. Many of the big names among us do, and look at what happens to them.

CHAPTER THIRTEEN

Satanic Visions

Within our ranks are servants of the enemy. Some of them are highly exalted, with vast television audiences. They not called by demon names, frightening everyone out of their minds. Instead, they are known as pastor or evangelist so and so, and are respected by all, just as Scripture said they would be.

> Jeremiah 5:31 The prophets prophesy falsely, And the priests rule by their *own* power; **and My people love *to have it* so!**

Why don't we discern them? Because they are pretty "close" to the truth, and we ourselves are not clinging single-heartedly to the Bible as our *only* infallible source for doctrine, Hosea 4:6. Many of these false prophets claim private interviews with Jesus, and other signs and wonders:

> Colossians 2:18 **...intruding into those things which he has not seen, vainly puffed up by his fleshly mind,**

Walking by sight, rather than by faith. The minute you hear of someone having a vision of Jesus, alarm bells ought to go off in your head, particularly if what that person teaches is not in line with Scripture. Here is why: If Jesus were to appear to one of these tel-evangelists today, the first thing He would tell that man would be to get his doctrine in line with the Bible! Now here's the point:

> **The church is not identifying the spirit behind the words these men are speaking! Instead, we are being dazzled by the supposed works they are performing.**

But works tell you nothing about the prophetic office. General Schwarzkopf did great works, but that didn't make him a prophet. According to Scripture, it's not the works we should be looking at, but the spiritual fruit, because Jesus said:

> Matthew 7:15-16 & Galatians 5:22-23 "Beware of false prophets, who come to you in sheep's clothing, but inwardly they are ravenous wolves. **You will know them by their fruits."** But the fruit of the Spirit is love, joy, peace, longsuffering, kindness, goodness, faithfulness, gentleness, self-control. Against such things there is no law.

As you know, Satan doesn't imitate the fruit of the Spirit very well, so false prophets can sometimes be recognized by rotten fruit. A spiteful attitude is rotten fruit. If someone is a true servant of God, he will bear good fruit. On a so-called Christian television network, one of the most acclaimed Pentecostal celebrities (we'll call him Benie) shared this little gem with his viewers:[112]

> "Somebody's attacking me because of something I'm teaching. Let me tell you something, brother: You watch it!... You know, I've looked for one verse in the Bible; I just can't seem to find it. One verse that said 'if you don't like them, kill them.' I really wish I could find it!... You stink, frankly that's the way I think about it!... Sometimes I wish God will give me a Holy Ghost machine gun; I'll blow your head off!"[113]

Abominable. Of course that 'anointed' Pentecostal luminary couldn't find a verse like that, or even close. It appears that he missed the

---

112 I have agonized about what is to follow, and have asked the Lord to help me to interpret His Word correctly, and to help me explain this spiritual battle accurately. I know the spiritual danger of exceeding what the Lord would have me write on this issue. We will all stand before God for what we say, but a Bible teacher has a special burden because he is responsible for the well-being of the souls he teaches, James 3:1. What follows could be written of many of today's church "leaders." Once you understand the guidelines of how to hold dubious fruit up against the straightedge of Scripture you should be able to insert the name of your choice.

113 Praise-a-thon Broadcast on TBN, November 8, 1990; as cited by John McArthur, *Charismatic Chaos,* (Grand Rapids, Zondervan) footnote, p14.

whole spiritual fruit message of the Bible. Only the god of this world sounds like that. The above threats against a Christian were made by a tel-evangelistic celebrity who claims to be "anointed" by the Holy Spirit to the absolute max. In this man's meetings, people are "slain in the spirit" by the hundreds, and multitudes are supposedly healed. But it is madness to believe that this man's "anointing" is of the Holy Spirit of God, because The Bible tells us plainly what Jesus' true servants are like:

> 2 Timothy 2:24-25...a servant of the Lord must not quarrel but be gentle to all, able to teach, patient, in humility correcting those who are in opposition, if God perhaps will grant them repentance, so that they may know the truth,

So whose spirit would lead this celebrity to display such a mean and aggressive nature? Could it be the Holy Spirit of God? Don't be ridiculous. That spirit was not the Spirit of peace, gentleness, mercy and brotherly kindness. It was the spirit of murder! A spirit so belligerent that one fears for the soul of the man who made those remarks, and for the souls of those he is enchanting. Contrast the Holy Spirit's voice with that celebrity's voice. The voice of Holy Spirit says:

> **1 John 3:14 We know that we have passed from death to life, because we love the brethren.**

> **1 John 3:15 Whoever hates his brother is a murderer, and you know that no murderer has eternal life abiding in him.**

But there is more. That celebrity's book, *Good Morning Holy Spirit,* is heresy by its very name![114] In the Bible we are directed to pray in (i.e. under the guidance of) the Holy Spirit. We are not directed to pray to the Holy Spirit, Ephesians 6:18. The Holy Spirit is He who enables us to communicate with Jesus. Jesus is the central figure of the Christian faith, so will the Holy Spirit lead us unto a spirit? The Lord Jesus' voice says:

---

114 Jesus clearly told us to whom we should direct our prayers: Matthew 11:28 Come to Me. all who are weary and heavy-laden. and I will give you rest. Matthew 6:9 "In this manner, therefore, pray: 'Our Father in heaven, Hallowed be your name.'" Nowhere in Scripture are we directed to pray to the Holy Spirit.

John 15:26, 16:13-14 But when the Helper comes, whom I shall send to you from the Father, the Spirit of truth who proceeds from the Father, **He will testify of Me...** when He, the Spirit of truth, has come... H**e will not speak on his own *authority*,** but whatever He hears, He will speak... **He will glorify me, for He will take of what is Mine and declare *it* to you.**

Do these charismatic false prophets lead people straight to the cross, as true Christians have done throughout the ages? It doesn't seem so. Instead, they are leading people to a spirit. According to John 15:26 and John 16:13-14, the real Holy Spirit leads you directly to Jesus; and following that, the Holy Spirit is GIVEN to you, Acts 5:32, Romans 5:5. Consequently, any man who leads you to a spirit would be going directly against what the Holy Spirit inspired the writers of the Bible to say... and it's tragic, not only for these leaders, but also for all who are listening to them. If a man goes against what the real Holy Spirit said in the Bible, and spiritual phenomena are still in evidence, whose spirit do you suppose is empowering that man?

2 Corinthians 11:14-15 ...For Satan himself transforms himself into an angel of light. **Therefore *it is* no great thing if his ministers also transform themselves into ministers of righteousness,** whose end will be according to their works.

Colossians 2:18-19 (excerpts) Let no one cheat you of your reward, taking delight in... **worship of angels... vainly puffed up by his fleshly mind, and not holding fast to the Head,** (Jesus is the head, Ephesians 1:22).

Are all those millions of misled people who are following these deceivers lost? Well, it is not for us to say; but if the verses about "Jesus' voice" mean anything at all, those millions are following the voice of a stranger.

John 10:27, John 10:5 "My sheep hear My voice, and I know them, and they follow Me. "Yet **they will by no means follow a stranger, but will flee from him,** for they do not know the voice of strangers."

We are to hold fast to Jesus. Going to a spirit is what the witch of Endor did, and that's what got Saul killed, 1 Samuel 28:19. "But evil men and impostors will grow worse and worse, deceiving and being deceived." 2 Timothy 3:13. Since we are commanded NOT to call up a spirit, will God's Spirit come to us if we call for Him? Don't be absurd. After salvation, the Holy Spirit continually indwells the heart of the believer, as many verses show.[115] He doesn't need to be called up. He already indwells us, *not just part way, but in full,* Colossians 2:9-10. If we don't accept that truth, and continue to call up a spirit, a spirit will come alright... but it won't be coming from above.

> Leviticus 20:27 A man or a woman who is a medium, or who has familiar spirits, shall surely be put to death; they shall stone them with stones. Their blood *shall be* upon them.

Now brethren, I am in no way against the Holy Spirit of God, nor any of His blessed and wonderful works; but these are demons we are calling up who are masquerading as the Holy Spirit! This isn't just some exquisitely thought out doctrinal point. These are real mind-bending evil spirits we are flirting with. Remember the story of Sally? Remember Rachel, Alvin, Fritz, Janice, and Charles the ex-satanist?

As Jesus said, "Enter by the narrow gate; for wide is the gate and broad is the way that leads to destruction, and there are many are who go in by it. Because narrow is the gate and difficult is the way which leads to life, and there are few who find it." Matthew 7:13-14. In one of his excellent little books, William McGrath of Minerva, OH, writes:

> "It is quite possible that the whole charismatic movement of our time is nothing more than a colossal religious swindle, a masterpiece of deception, doctrines of demons in which an apparent 'spiritual renewal' is simply a drawing together of what has been called *The Three Sisters:* Evangeline (the Protestants), Charisma (the Pentecostals), and Roma (the Catholics)."[116]

Well, what about all these claimed "anointings?" Is all this a sham? One of the most misused words in the church today is "anointing." We hear of this person being "anointed" to preach, or of that person

---

115 Isaiah 57:15; John 7:38, 14:16-17, 15:26, 16:7; Acts 5:32, Romans 5:5, 8:1, 8:16; 1 Corinthians 3:16, 6:19; 2 Corinthian 1:22, 6:16; Galatians 3:2, 4:6; Ephesians 1:13, 4:30; 1 Thessalonians 4:8; 2 Thessalonians 2:13; 2 Timothy 1:7; Titus 3:5; I John 2:20,3:24.

116 William R. McGrath, *How Superstitious Preaching Spreads Panic,* (Minerva, OH, Christian Printing Mission, 1992), pp13-14.

being "anointed" to heal. These claims of special "anointings" take our eyes off Jesus and put them on a man.

> Isaiah 8:19-20 And when they say to you, "Seek those who are mediums and wizards, who whisper and that mutter," should not a people seek their God?...
> **To the law and to the testimony! If they do not speak according to this word, it is because there is no light in them.**

Isaiah says, don't go after the miracle workers; go to the Word of God. Any "anointing" that brings glory to some "wizard" is not biblical. When the Holy Spirit anoints someone, Jesus gets the glory! In fact, that is one of the tests for a false prophet: Who is getting the glory? Whose name is up in lights? Jesus' or the man's? The Holy Spirit's office is to lead us straight to Jesus, with no side detours through someone's "anointing!"

> Jeremiah 17:5 Thus says the LORD: "Cursed is the man who trusts in man And makes flesh his strength, Whose heart departs from the LORD.

When the Holy Spirit really anoints, like He did at Pentecost, miraculous things happen that can be verified: Mighty winds and tongues of fire, Acts 2:3, Acts 11:15. Houses shaking, Acts 4:15. People were not just "slain in the spirit," they were slain dead as a hammer, Acts 5:1-11... and *Jesus got the glory!* Seen any "anointings" like that lately? Any mighty winds... houses shaking... tongues of fire? No? Well don't feel bad, neither have I. However, similar signs have taken place during the Christian Era. Here is what happened in Holland in AD1555:

> ...the Waterland brethren, on account of the severe persecution, could not live in houses, but had to keep themselves in boats and in the fields, because they knew not where to hide themselves from the constables, who were looking for them everywhere, and sought their lives. It was at this time that six brethren, who were together in a boat, were apprehended in the Oostsaner field, and brought to Amsterdam, where they were sentenced to death. It was in the beginning of the winter when they were brought in the Volewijk, and all strangled at the stake. There was freezing weather for thirteen weeks from this time on, and, what is remarkable, during all these thirteen weeks a light like a candle

> stood over each stake to which the bodies of the six brethren were fastened, and burned all night.
>
> ...The persons who saw this...were...pious and credible persons, who related it to many, in order that this miracle should never be forgotten, but be remembered, to the edification of the pious.[117]

Now that's an anointing! "Precious in the sight of the Lord is the death of His godly ones," Psalm 116:15. I am not sure that the Lord did not permit some of these dearest of brethren to die so that we, 400 years later, could see the difference between His sovereign hand, and the deceptions of the enemy. The false prophets haven't figured out a way to counterfeit tongues of fire yet, but if they find one, they'll probably use it:

> 2 Peter 2:18-19 For when they speak great swelling *words* of emptiness, they allure through the lusts of flesh, through lewdness, the ones who have actually escaped from those who live in error. While they promise them liberty, they themselves are slaves of corruption;

As a sad but interesting note, after the miracles recorded in the Christian Era were performed, there wasn't anyone left standing around who could crow about his "anointing." It seems that every spectacular miracle (recorded after the apostolic era) was performed by some dear saint who was being martyred for the sake of the Lord Jesus. But just like John the Baptist, that is as it should be. Not the dear brethren, but Christ Jesus Himself gets the glory.

Some critic might say that some of the miracles in church records would not pass a legal test for evidence. In a couple of instances that may be true. But these accounts were written by brethren being tortured and burned alive for Jesus' sake. Truth is what they died for. If they were willing to be burned at the stake for refusing to accept the false doctrines of the Roman Church, rest assured, their followers wouldn't lie about how they died.

Other Christian authors have written many books that expose the egregious heresies and blasphemies of today's Charismatic, Third Wave, Word-Faith and Vineyard movements; and on the horizon there are worse heresies still, going so far beyond scriptural truth that what

---

117 Thieleman J. van Braght, *Martyrs Mirror,* (Scottdale, PA, Herald Press, 1950) p568.

they teach can no longer be called Christianity.[118] These other writers report a tragedy of monumental proportions. The Lord predicted it, but it is still a tragedy, not only for the deluded Charismatic leaders themselves, but also for all the souls they carry off into error with them:

> 2 John 1:9-11 Whoever transgresses and does not abide in the doctrine of Christ does not have God. He who abides in the doctrine of Christ has both the Father and the Son. **If anyone comes to you and does not bring this doctrine, do not receive him into your house nor greet him; for he who greets him shares in his evil deeds.**

Very soon, the saints will again need to separate themselves from "the blasphemy by those who say they are Jews and are not, but are a synagogue of Satan," Revelation 2:9. In these last days, we will need to be vigilant as never before in our stand against satanic deception from within our own ranks. Jesus said, "Night cometh," and if we look around us with our eyes open, we can see that a spiritual night is already covering our land. Verbal attacks against the brethren can be seen nightly, prime time, on national TV networks. Many saints are being shunned, while others are being harassed and are losing their jobs for the sake of Jesus' name. Physical persecution cannot be far behind.

In Nazi Germany, it was the Jews who were killed. In this country, it will be the Christians and the Jews. That sounds improbable, I know. But just seven years after the Nazis came to power, millions of naked men, women, and children were being herded into gas chambers. A murderous adversary lurks beneath the thin veneer of every civilization, and through sadistic movies and satanic rock he has captured the hearts and minds of our children. On whose side will they be when they begin to rule in the land?

> Micah 7:6 For son dishonors father, Daughter rises against her mother, Daughter-in-law against her mother-in-law; **A man's enemies *are* the men of his own household.**

---

118 John McArthur, *Charismatic Chaos,* (Grand Rapids, Zondervan, 1992). Dave Hunt, *The Seduction of Christianity,* (Eugene, OR, Harvest House, 1988)

Revelation 12:17 And the dragon was enraged with the woman, and he went to make war with the rest of her offspring, who keep the commandments of God *(the Jews)* and have to the testimony of Jesus Christ *(the Christians)*.

Each individual saint will need to guard his own soul and the souls of his family, against the ever louder and more strident assaults of the enemy, 2 Peter 3:17. How? By clinging to the Bible. Put your trust in God's Word. It is a haven of truth amidst a sea of lies. It is a mighty fortress against the deceits of the enemy. The doctrines of demons, and turning aside to myths predicted for the last days sound good, and we're feeling good, but Scripture says:

Matthew 24:24 For false christs and **false prophets will rise and show great signs and wonders** to deceive, if possible, even the elect.

2 Timothy 4:3-4 For the time will come when they will not endure sound doctrine, but according to their own desires, *because* they have itching ears, they will heap up for themselves teachers; and they will tum *their* ears away from the truth, and be turned aside to fables.

2 Thessalonians 2:10-12 ...they did not receive the love of the truth, that they might be saved. And for this reason God will send them strong delusion, that they should believe the lie, that they all may be condemned who did not believe the truth but had pleasure in unrighteousness.

2 Peter 3:17, Mark 13:9 You therefore, beloved, since you know *this* beforehand, **beware lest you also fall from your own steadfastness, being led away with the error of the wicked;** ....for they will deliver you up to councils, and you will be beaten in the synagogues. You will be brought before rulers and kings for My sake, for a testimony to them.

CHAPTER FOURTEEN

Facing Reality

We can continue to play with evil spirits and doctrines of demons if we want to, but the end thereof is death, not only in this world, but for some, in the world to come, 1 Timothy 4:1. If we are not frightened by our tampering with the occult, it shows a heart condition almost beyond help, "the sin unto death!" 1 John 5:16. As one looks out over the churches, we see many poor souls who have turned aside to spiritism. They run around incanting, "Praise you Jesus," with hands uplifted, while disobedience is in their hearts:

> Ezekiel 13:17 "Likewise, son of man, **set your face against the daughters of your people, who prophesy out of their own heart;** prophesy against them...

We don't need to go to some witches' coven in a major city to find demonic activity. Women of the local churches are flitting from hangnails to cancer, laying on hands, and saying in a fit of mediumistic fervor, "Be healed in the name of Jesus!" saying "in the name of Jesus" does not sanctify open defiance.[119] We have scriptural examples of what happened to people who tried for more spiritual authority than God granted them by law. In addition to Korah, Numbers 16, the sons of Sceva tried exorcism, in Jesus' name, without themselves being submitted to the Lord. The demons attacked them.

---

119 1 Timothy 2:11, James 5:14

Acts 19:13-16 Then some of the itinerant Jewish exorcists took it upon themselves to call the name of the Lord Jesus over those who had evil spirits, saying, "We exorcise you by the Jesus whom Paul preaches." Also there were seven sons of Sceva, a Jewish chief priest, who did so. And the evil spirit answered and said, "Jesus I know, and Paul I know; but who are you?" Then the man in whom the evil spirit was leaped on them, overpowered them, and prevailed against them, so that they fled out of that house naked and wounded.

With their husband's approval, Christian women are also in *open* and *direct disobedience* to the submission statutes, "keep silent... receive instruction in all quiet submissiveness... cover her head... not exercise authority..." Yesterday, today, and always, sick Christians are commanded to *call the elders!* The elders have been given biblical authority to heal. God will not short-circuit *His own* delegated authorities. If God healed through one of these women, He would be placing His stamp of approval on their disobedience of His Word. That He will not do! That a woman may not be an elder is apparent from Scripture.[120]

Ezekiel 13:23 "Therefore you shall no longer envision futility nor practice divination; for I will deliver My people out of your hand..."

Those are the laws, and Satan knows it. In ignoring them, women have given the enemy access to demonize what they do. Why would Satan give someone the idea that they could heal in Jesus' name? To break down the authority of God's delegated elders, to discredit the Bible, and to lead us into rebellion. So without anyone noticing it, the great apostasy has come upon us.[121]

---

120 1 Timothy 3:1-7 and Titus 1:5-9.

121 This in no wise means that women can't pray for the sick. Christians of both genders have been praying for the brethren, with the Lord's wonderful blessing, all the way back to the apostle Paul's time; and many brethren have been healed. But there is a vast difference between pleading for the Lord's mercy, and claiming that you have been granted the miraculous power to heal. The first is godly, the second is insolent presumption. With the exception of the apostles themselves, there is not one confirmed example, in all church history, of anyone whom the Lord so empowered.

Isaiah 3:12 *As for* My people, children *are* their oppressors, And women rule over them. O my people! Those who lead you cause *you* to *err*, And destroy the way of your paths.

When this book was begun, it appeared that just a few of the charismatic phenomena were demonic. Recognizing that there are rare exceptions, it now appears that most are. In the demonic phenomena recorded here, and in many not mentioned, it seems that the persons involved were in some way giving Satan access to their lives, either through some open sin, or because the submission ordinance and related statutes were ignored. That is sin, too. Sometimes, a foothold was granted by knowing and understanding these commands, but continuing to worship and fellowship in churches that disobey them. That is just like Saul holding the cloaks of those who stoned Stephen, Acts 7:58. The enemy is not blind. Even by man's law that makes one an accomplice. Satan doesn't need a super-highway. A little chink in the armor will do just fine.

Through false doctrine or intimidation, members of many charismatic congregations pressure others to exhibit the same spiritual phenomena they do.[122] A Baptist pastor in Mississippi tells of an experience that took place after he had spoken to a group of Full Gospel Christian Businessmen:

After my sermon, men of the group surrounded me and said, "That was great, preacher. Now all you really need is to be filled with the Spirit and start speaking in tongues."

"If that is what the Lord had in mind for me, let's go for it," I said. So they surrounded me, laid hands on me, and started praying over me in tongues. Nothing happened.

Then they coached me in a few "tongue words," and prayed over me some more. Still nothing happened, and they appeared a little distressed. I said, "Look fellows, if the Holy Spirit wants me to speak in tongues, I don't need to prime the pump by mumbling something unintelligible, so I'm not going to do that." Then they suggested that I

122 Some Pentecostals, claiming to be filled with the spirit, look down on those who do not speak in tongues, considering them to be "less spiritual." I personally know one Pentecostal woman who believes that she has become so spiritual that she has outgrown her need to read or study the Bible.

hum, to kind of get me started, and they began to pray over me in earnest.[123]

Here I was, a grown man, going "Hummm... Hummm" with all these other grown men standing around me muttering something or other while I'm humming. So while I'm going "Hummm... Hummm," I began to get tickled at the situation, and started laughing uproariously. I couldn't help myself.

The other men got real excited and joyous and said, "Wow, look at that, he's laughing in the Spirit." When I finally gained my composure and told them what was really going on, they got pretty irritated with me.

That sounds like a funny story, but there isn't anything humorous about it. It could have ended in that pastor's spiritual deception. Many a man would not have been so analytical about what was happening in his heart, and one more pastor could have been deluded into believing that he had been "filled with the Spirit," and gone forth to teach that doctrine in his church. That sort of thing actually happens. If we are not diligent about walking in the truth, it's very easy to spiritually delude ourselves. Phoebe Kinkaid of North Dakota faked some of her charismatic experiences rather than have her friends think she was not "spiritual" enough. Thank the Lord for this dear sister who had the courage to come forth:

There is probably not a charismatic anywhere who will tell you what I am about to. While I was in the movement I exhibited all the "gifts," speaking in tongues, of being "slain" (we called it resting) in the spirit, discernment, teaching and prophecy. While I was "slain" in the spirit, I was never really out cold; but with everyone else falling to the floor around you, you felt pretty stupid if you're the only one left standing.

While I was in the movement I seemed to be happy, with many ministries in the church; but upon reflection, it was a false joy. Here is how I know. Along-time friend and sister in the Lord lied about me. I felt betrayed and my joy vanished. I was deeply hurt, and full of bitterness of spirit. In spite of all my "gifts," forgiveness was impossible.

In contrast, when I left the error of that movement, recognized my position in Jesus, was baptized, and started covering my head, I experienced real JOY! Not like before at all, but rooted in my very soul, and the Lord gave me a forgiving heart. Suddenly, it was easy to forgive my friend, and many others who had wronged me far, far worse.

---

123 Yoga practitioners also have a routine during which they hum.

If I had been in the movement for only a short time, I could be mistaken about its true spiritual nature, but I was a leader, a woman "elder" if you please, for nearly four years. I was invited to other churches to "teach" people how to open themselves up to the spirit. I would lay hands on people and see them fall over (no big deal when you know what is going on). Sometimes I had spiritual insights about others in the group, given to me by the enemy no doubt, to validate my "ministry." Scary, isn't it? I thank the Lord Jesus daily for. delivering me from that great deception.

I feel sorry for my former brethren in the charismatic movement. They have to go for their weekly "fix" of praising and singing for hours, just to get pumped up so they can face the week ahead.

Then there is a dear, stalwart sister who worships in a charismatic church in the black community. She is silent in the assembly and wears a head-covering. She stands alone for Jesus. Get this: the "tongue-speaking" ladies of the church gang up on her, point at her covering, and pressure her with, "You are resisting the spirit." Now whose spirits do you suppose she is resisting by wearing a head-covering and remaining silent? Not the Holy Spirit of God, surely.

On being Filled

We have just seen how *not* to be filled with the Spirit, so how do we obey "be filled with the Spirit" as Ephesians 5:18 commands? Because of its simplicity, it is unbelievable that there are saints who don't know how. It's easy. Just let the Holy Spirit fulfill in your life the functions that He was sent here by Jesus to perform! The Holy Spirit will surely accomplish what He was sent here to do. Jesus told us plainly what the Spirit's role would be in John 14 through 16. Simply stated, and without getting into a lengthy theological explanation, the Holy Spirit will:

1. **Teach you all things: Read your Bible!**
2. **Reprove the world of sin: Witness!**
3. **Lead us to righteousness: Clean up your life!**

When we receive power of the Holy Spirit, it will be to accomplish those three things. The Holy Spirit's office is to glorify and witness for Jesus in the world, in our hearts, and to bring us – God's children – into conformity to the image of His Son, Romans 8:29. If we allow the Holy Spirit to perform His stated offices through us, then we will suddenly, and unexpectedly, find ourselves filled with the Holy Spirit! You see why, don't you? The Holy Spirit will fill those who are engaged in the activities He was sent here to perform.

The Holy Spirit was sent to lead people to Jesus, and to comfort and correct the saints!

That is so elementary, how do we miss it? If we are obedient, if we let Him function in the way the Bible tells us He was sent to function; then maybe, He *might* give us one of the "greater" gifts. But if He does so, that gift will *still* be to assist us to fulfill the functions He came here to perform, and to bring glory to God's Son. It is up to Him. He knows our hearts.

I know of several men whom the Lord has used in miraculous ways in the last decade, but they would be greatly offended if I were to share their names. One withered boy was healed through a missionary, and the boy's family didn't even know the missionary's name. All the little boy's father knew was that Jesus had healed his son. It was indeed Jesus who did the healing, so isn't that the way it's supposed to be?

A Few Final Notes

Some have wondered whether head-covering, and women under authority, is an ordinance of the same importance as baptism and communion. A reasonable question. Let's ask: Is baptism more important than communion? It doesn't appear to be. All of God's Word is inspired, and "Man shall not live by bread alone, but by *every word* that proceeds from the mouth of God," Matthew 4:4. All of God's ordinances are stated as firm commands, so to please the Lord, our obedience to His Word cannot be selective:

Baptism is a symbol of our burial and resurrection with Christ Jesus.

Communion is a symbol of our identification with the cross of Christ.

Head-covering and women under authority are symbols of the sovereignty of God, His government, the defeat of Satan, the salvation of the soul, and the headship of Christ over the church.

Many sisters have asked how big, and of what, should a head-covering be made? The Greek word *katakalupto_* (Strong's No.2619g, defined: to cover up), used in 1 Corinthians 11:5-6, implies a veil, something "coming down over" the head. Scripture tells us no more than that, so neither will the author. There are no verses on material or color. Over the years, various groups have mandated various styles, colors and materials, and those traditions have stood them well. But whatever you wear, it should be obvious that your covering is not for fashion's sake. It is "for the angels," and they're not influenced by what is in vogue.

Is a head-covering to be worn during church only, or if not, for how many hours of the day should a woman's head be covered? Well, Scripture states, "...when praying or prophesying." Many sisters pray throughout the day, and a woman's head should be covered any time she prays. Some churches advocate a covering except when sleeping, and we know one brother who was relieved of devilish dreams after his wife started wearing a nightcap.

Men and boys are not permitted to cover their heads. Only women and girls can. Since a wife is one flesh with her husband, she has the privilege and responsibility of showing to the angels the spiritual position of her whole family. Surely, dear sister, you would want that head-covering to be noticeable enough so that both sides would know that your soul, and the souls of the family you represent belong to Jesus!

How silent is silence? Women not speaking or holding forth on doctrinal truths *(while the church is assembled as a mixed congregation)* is mandated by Scripture. Neither may they question what is taught while in church 1 Corinthians 14:34-35. If that passage is interpreted in the strictest sense, silence would include singing, and being members of the choir. There are brethren who hold so sober a view, and one would be hard-pressed to call it error. These are strict and exact statutes, but we did not write the rules, and it is not up to the clay to tell the Potter what He should do.

What can women scripturally do in the church? They can perform any function that does not break a type of Christ and the church. This includes teaching other women and children. In fact, that is probably what 1 Timothy 2:15 is all about:

> 1 Timothy 2:15 Nevertheless she will be saved in childbearing if they continue in faith, love, and holiness, with self-control.

What will be preserved? This verse certainly isn't about salvation; it appears in a passage about women's position in the church. As a result, it seems that through children, a woman's *ministry* will be preserved. In 2 Timothy 1:5-6 we read that Paul credits Timothy's mother and grandmother for his "sincere faith." But they taught him as a boy, and at home. They didn't preach to him from the pulpit!

Christian wife, do you have an unsaved husband? Obey 1 Peter 3:1-2. Note "...they, without a word, may be won..." Many unsaved husbands are not led to the Lord because some militant wife, believing she is doing God's will by beating her husband over the head with the Bible, has instead driven him away. The author's wife won him back to the Lord by being subject to that Scripture. He could find no fault in her. His now being in full-time Christian service is in great part the fruit of that dear woman's selfless service. As is true for us all, if women today would do exactly what God's Word says, their efforts for Him would bear the *most* fruit.

What about women "pastors" or church leaders who do take authority over men? Sometimes their ministry seems to be blessed. Church history clearly shows that God's governmental judgment will fall on churches with women in authority. They will have a deluding spirit, leading to false doctrine and eventual apostasy. Many sects and splinter groups were either begun, or strongly influenced, by women: Christian Science, the Shakers, the Seventh Day Adventists, the Methodists, the Pentecostals and others. The greatest example of them all being the deification of the Virgin Mary by the Roman papacy.

In some mainline Protestant denominations, both male and female "pastors" are now teaching precepts so humanistic that people cannot come to a saving knowledge of the Lord Jesus through what they preach. Women "theologians" are calling our sovereign God "a Baker woman God," and are re-translations the Bible to weaken the doctrine of His masculine nature.[124] In their feminism, they blaspheme. Jesus said, "I and My Father" (not I and my neuter) "are one." Just another strange contortion that Satan has led the church to take when it departed from God's Word and ignored His governmental order.

Isaiah 29:13 ...these people draw near with their mouths And honor Me with their lips, **But have removed their hearts far from Me, And their fear toward Me is taught by the commandment of men,**

---

124 *That's Outrageous,* Readers Digest, Oct 1992, p127 col.1

But despite all this "spiritual wickedness in high places," it's still a truth battle. Jesus won the power struggle on the cross. It is a fight against the traditions of man and the deceptions of the enemy. It was Gospel truth that changed the Roman Empire. That same truth can change the world today:

> Matthew 10:16 & 28:20 "Behold, I send you out as sheep in the midst of wolves. Therefore be wise as serpents and harmless as doves... "Teaching them to observe all things that I have commanded you; and lo, I am with you always, *even* to the end of the age." Amen.

Most of us think we are powerless because we don't have seminary training, or are not behind a pulpit. That's just as big a lie of the devil now as it has always been. The apostle Paul didn't start out as the pastor of a large Gentile church either. Power is not in the Christian's position in the church; power is in the truth! The minute you are willing to put yourself on the line for the truth of the Bible, its power will become abundantly evident to you. The enemy will come against you in all his lying force. During the whole Christian Era, not one single martyr died for going along with the crowd, so...

> **Obey the head-covering ordinance** (and associated commands), **and you will stir up the forces of darkness that are attacking your church, and be up to your neck in a spiritual battle!**

If you still think that's a joke, just try it. If you really want to stand for Jesus, here's your chance. Now that you understand what head-covering is all about, you can be a bastion against the forces of darkness, no matter how unimportant you consider yourself to be. By obeying these commands, and without saying a word to anyone, you will personally be in the battle!

But don't think it will be easy. If people think you are wearing that covering for style, they will leave you alone; but the minute they discover that you're doing it for Jesus, you'll get ridicule and verbal abuse, and you'll find your friends deserting you. That is the way the Lord said it would be, 2 Timothy 3:12, and that's how you'll know you're doing something right:[125]

---

125 Matthew 5:11-12 "Blessed are you when they revile and persecute you, and say all kinds of evil against you falsely for my sake. Rejoice and be exceedingly glad, for great *is* your reward in heaven, for so they persecuted the prophets who were before you.

> Heb 11:7 By faith Noah, being divinely warned of things not yet seen, moved with godly fear, prepared an ark for the saving of his household, **by which he condemned the world** and became heir of the righteousness which is according to faith.

And that is exactly what you will be doing. Condemning the god of this world who caused the fall of man. I implore you, stand for the Word of God. Stand for Jesus. There are very few today who will. Compromise is everywhere, and many will try to lead you away from what is written here. Please don't let them, because Jesus can use you, whoever you are.

I knew a Bible teacher once, long ago, who was a drunken profligate. He was bound by the worst sort of sordid immorality and wickedness; sins that sometimes accompany alcoholism, and "the hidden things of shame." 2 Corinthians 4:2. Though he was teaching the Bible honestly, not in anyone's wildest dreams could it be said that he was walking with the Lord while he was in such abominable sin. Then the Lord reached down and changed that man's sinful heart.

Strangely enough, since the Lord cleansed that degenerate brother, he is one of the few men I know in Christian service who is willing to stand on the whole Word of God with a humble heart. He was forgiven much, and loves much Luke 7:47. But, if that ex-libertine is any example of the few willing warriors the Lord has left, then surely there is little hope... for that wretched man was I.

There is a point to telling my story. If God can forgive and still use me despite my appalling past, what is your excuse? What is there in your life that you think. the God of heaven cannot forgive, or cannot cleanse through the blood of the Lord Jesus, His perfect sacrifice, His blessed Son? Come to Him this minute, my friend. Come to Him who died for you. Get on your face before God and ask forgiveness for your sins. Learn of Him from His wonderful and eternal Word, and go forth in the power of His might. Maybe the Lord would still withhold the devastation that He has decreed upon our land. For even as we look about us, this wicked country crumbles. As the malignant cancer of gross heresy spreads, we behold the death of the church. We are the pallbearers of the truths for which the martyrs died. We stand by, wringing our hands, as the god of this world buries the Gospel of Jesus Christ in the muck of ungodliness. We have lost the fortitude of John Hooper... the faith of Augustine the baker... the strength of Leonhard Keyser... the courage of that young Englishman... the anointing of those six nameless brethren strangled at the stake. We have forgotten how to walk with God.

Could God heal? Of course! But many will say in their hearts, "This message is not for me, but for that cold-hearted church down the street," and fire will again consume. This time though, the fire comes for us, 2 Peter 3:7-10. There are those who will find convoluted, counter-scriptural ways around what is written here, and they will find multitudes to agree with them. Some false prophet again will play the flute (probably via satellite) and all will dance, Matthew 11:17.

But keeping our heads in the sand will not delay the coming storm. The Lord predicted judgment on an unrighteous Israel in too many Scriptures to count. All they had was the Old Testament. The church has the whole Bible, the whole counsel of God, and we shall not escape. God's Word will stand:

Thus says the LORD of hosts:
"Do not listen to the words of the prophets
who prophesy to you.
They make you worthless;
They speak a vision of their own heart,
Not from the mouth of the LORD.
They continually say to those who despise Me,
'The LORD has said, "You shall have peace"';
And to everyone who walks according to the dictates
of his own heart,
they say, 'No evil shall come upon you.'"

For who has stood in the council of the LORD,
And has perceived and heard His word?
Who has marked His word and heard *it*?
Behold, a whirlwind of the LORD has gone forth in fury –
a violent whirlwind!
It will fall violently on the head of the wicked.
The anger of the LORD will not tum back
Until He has executed and performed the thoughts of His heart.

In the latter days you will understand it perfectly.

I have not send these prophets,
yet they ran.
I have not spoken to them,

> yet they prophesied.
> But if they had stood in My council,
> And had caused My people to hear My words,
> Then they would have turned them from their evil way
> And from the evil of their doings."
>
> Jeremiah 23:16-22

The end is almost upon us now. We are only prophetic seconds from the end, and the clock is ticking. Bible prophecy is now open for us to understand, if anybody still cares, or is looking. But the church today is neither hot nor cold, just lukewarm, like Jesus said it would be. He will spit it out of His mouth as He declared He would Revelation 3:16.[126] In Europe today, less than 3% of the population is Christian, and that is dwindling. The great cathedrals are empty. The flame flickers there, and spiritual darkness cloaks the land, John 9:4. In our own country, the church is so worldly that saint cannot be told from sinner. Night has fallen here, too, but we'll keep dancing. Some cry for revival, but it won't come. Too few are willing to pay the price for it – a broken-hearted repentance before the Lord and submission to His Word.

"Oh, that You would rend the heavens!
That you would and come down!
That the mountains might shake
at Your presence –

"Nevertheless,
when the Son of Man comes,
will He really find faith
on the earth?"

Isaiah 64:1 & Luke 18:8

---

126 Ellis H. Skolfield, *Hidden Beast 2,* (P.O. Box 453, Fort Myers, FL 33902, Fish House, 1991)

All this is so plain in Scripture, Why haven't we heard it before? Well it's been in the Bible all along, but those 17 excuses have clouded the truth. There are some pastors who have seen these truths but are afraid to teach them. "Those verses don't preach," they say; "They're too unpopular, and people would leave my church." Woe to those who take a hireling's pay and do not teach the truth.

Others have worried that the somber warnings in this book might prevent someone from receiving a spiritual gift which the Lord intends to give him. That's laughable. A few feeble words by mortal man could not stop the Lord from giving a spiritual gift to whomever He wills. God is the Lord, El Shaddai, the Almighty, who does exactly as He determines. On the other hand, if this little book keeps just one soul from being demonized through these false gifts, it was worth the effort. Throughout this book, the author has tried to show the contrast between true Christianity, and a false religion of the same name, which has taken its place. Pseudo-Christians "worship" God because of what God can do for them. We brazenly appear before the throne of grace of a Holy God, demanding gifts, that we may boast in the flesh.

> James 4:3 You ask and do not receive, because you ask amiss, that you may spend *it* on your pleasures.

That "form of godliness" is not God-centered; it is man-centered. It is not Christianity; it is humanism, and it pervades the church. God's true servants worship God, regardless of the outcome. A true servant will worship God, even if all he ever gets out of it is suffering. Why? Because the Lord Jesus is worthy of worship, Revelation 4:11; 5:12. He is holy and righteous and pure and true and just and merciful and love. He is all things good, and in Him there is no darkness at all. He is totally worthy of our worship. If we worship the Creator of the universe for any reason other than who He is, it is self-serving, and man-centered. It is humanism.

But despite the humanism and spiritual excesses you have read about in this book, the Lord, by his Spirit, is still working through His servants. Souls are being saved. Souls are being saved, and the sick are being healed in the name of Jesus. Holy angels have appeared to some, and miracles have happened to others. So where is the balance? How do we relate to the blessed work of God's Spirit, without departing from the teachings of Christ (2 John 9) and venturing off into spiritism?

The answer lies in maintaining a bond-servant relationship with the Lord Jesus as He has revealed Himself to us in Scripture: To obey Him with a whole heart, no matter how unpopular the command. To seek to know "Christ Jesus, and Him crucified for the remission of sins." To stop worrying about ourselves (and our possible "gifts"), and to fulfill the work the Lord left the church on earth to do. To love and serve the Lord with a whole heart, even if at the end of it, we were to still go to hell. Until we are willing to take that firm a stand, we are not serving the Lord; we are just serving ourselves.

The martyr didn't die because of all the good things the Lord did for them in the flesh. They were not killed because they lay down in front of abortion clinics, or were protecting the environment. they were murdered because they taught the truth of the Gospel. "For the weapons of our warfare are not carnal but mighty in God for pulling down strongholds..." 2 Corinthians 10:4. When Christians first evangelized the world, it was not the miracles they performed, but the truths they preached that changed the Roman Empire. It was not their tongues, nor physical healings that transformed men's hearts, but the miracle of a risen Savior. It was the Gospel of Jesus Christ, and that is the truth upon which our hearts should still be fixed:

> Luke 9:60 & John 6:63 Jesus said to him, "Let the dead bury their own dead, **but you go and preach the kingdom of God."** "The words that I speak to you are spirit, and *they* are life."

The moment the last of Jesus' lost sheep comes into the fold, He will return, and the time is short. One dear brother, on his knees before the Lord because of the "abominations in our midst," was quickened by the Spirit to give thanks to the Lord for this present time of peace: because right now is the best time we shall ever see, in an ever-descending spiral of godlessness and violence. Thank God that the days of waiting are almost over for us, and for the saints before the throne who cease not to cry out, saying: "How long, O Lord, holy and true, until you judge and avenge our blood on those who dwell on the earth?" Revelation 6:10

All the entries in *Fox's Book of Martyrs*, and *Martyr's Mirror*, have not been written yet. Beloved brethren, suffering still, will yet lay down their lives for Jesus' sake, by torture and by fire. But have not Jesus' sheep stood tallest when all seemed hopeless from the viewpoint of this present world?

> Revelation 22:11-14 "He who is unjust, let him be unjust still; he who is filthy, let him be filthy still; he who is righteous, let him be righteous still; he who is holy, let him be holy still. And behold, I am coming quickly, and My reward *is* with Me, to give to everyone according to his work. I and the Alpha and the Omega, *the* Beginning and *the* End, the First and the Last. Blessed *are* those who do His commandments, that they may have the right to the tree of life, and may enter through the gates into the city."

"You shall also
take a small number of them
and bind them in the edge
of your *garment*."

Ezekiel 5:3

Postscript

to the Reprinted 2024 Edition

At first blush, the reader may have taken this book for the standard critique of Charismatic "Full Gospel" groups who seek a "second work of grace", or "baptism of the Holy Spirit" that is evidenced by various blessings such as speaking in "tongues", miraculous healings, being "slain in the spirit", and the casting out of demons. In a kind of Divine irony, it is the churches that teach the biblical doctrine of the infilling of the Holy Spirit concurrent with the new birth, that are teaching a true "Full Gospel."

Anabaptist readers, on the other hand, might read this book, somewhat smugly perhaps, with a narrow focus on how the wearing of a woman's head covering is emphasized, and by a Protestant at that.

Neither view is entirely incorrect, but the focus of each of those views is much too narrow. The studious reader will have noticed these three principle points that are central to the whole book:

1. All Christians who practice a life of obedience have the indwelling of the Holy Spirit, without demanding a "second work of grace," or "Baptism of the Holy Spirit." Demons have no control over such a believer. "For you are the temple of the living God." 2 Corinthians 6:16. "And we are His witnesses to these things, and *so* also *is* the Holy Spirit whom God has given to those who obey Him." Acts 5:32

2. Disobedience leads to the grieving of the Holy Spirit, and persistence in disobedience leads to the departure of the Holy Spirit.

3. Without the indwelling of the Holy Spirit, the individual is susceptible to demonic influences. Absent the Holy Spirit, an individual is not in a spiritual vacuum, but may eventually become possessed by demons. Matthew 12:43, Luke 11:24

Anabaptists may tend to think of demon possession as something that only happens in far-away places to jungle-dwelling pagan tribes that practice various idolatries; or in any case, to "worldly" unbelievers, practicing occultists, or witches. The thought that this could happen within Anabaptist circles is unthinkable – or is it? It has been said that "nature abhors a vacuum", and it is even more certain that there is no such thing as a sustainable spiritual vacuum.

The Bible offers no hint of any geographical boundaries that demons will respect, nor any other exceptions because of one's denominational affiliation, faithful ancestors, cultural customs, ministry positions, or anything else. God is no respecter of persons. As the Apostle Peter put it, "In truth I perceive that God shows no partiality." (Acts 10:34) Let us take this warning to heart.

"They sow to the wind, And reap the whirlwind." Hosea 8:7

Finis